Kansas City's
UNION STATION
Reflections After 100 Years

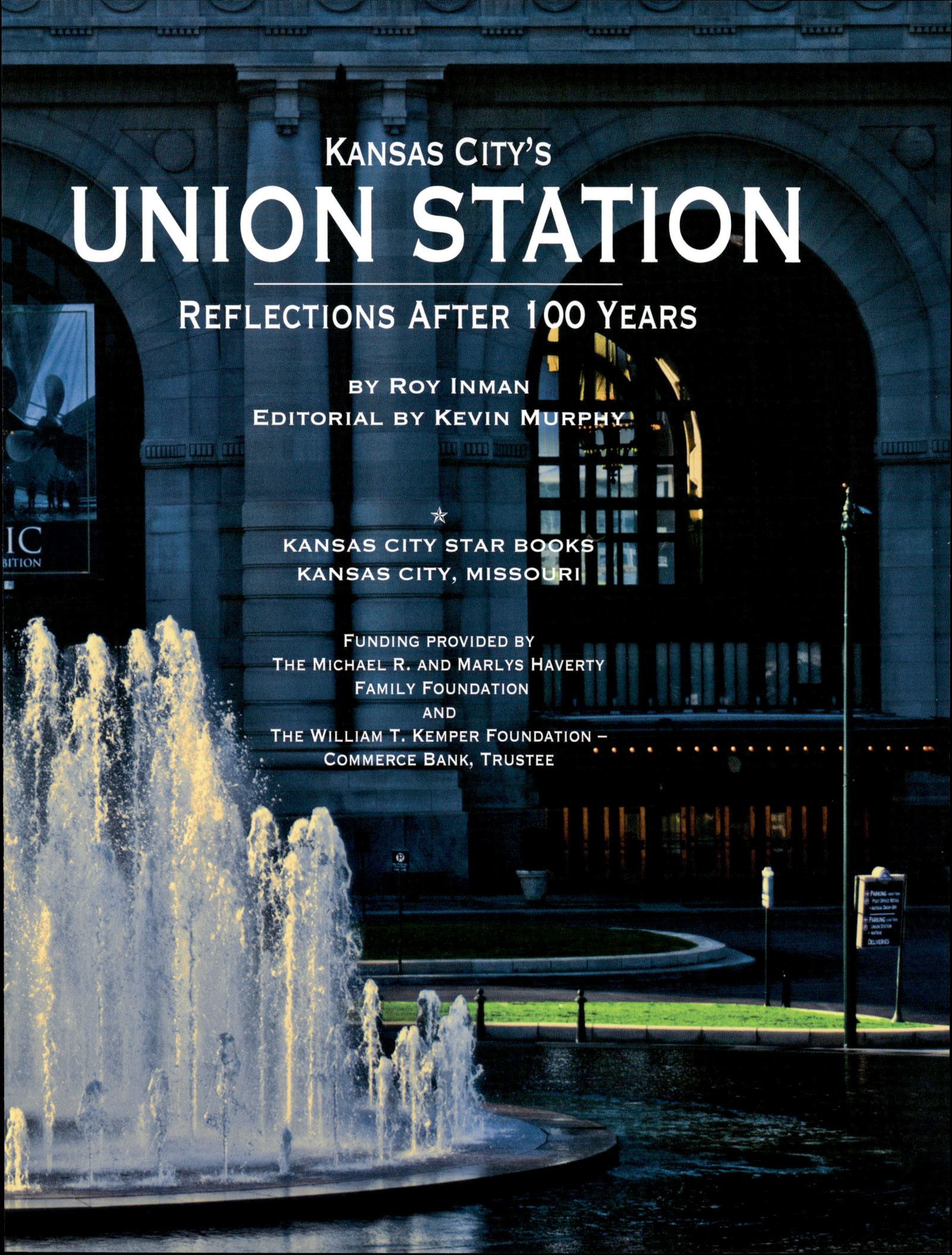

Kansas City's
UNION STATION

Reflections After 100 Years

by Roy Inman
Editorial by Kevin Murphy

✦

KANSAS CITY STAR BOOKS
KANSAS CITY, MISSOURI

Funding provided by
The Michael R. and Marlys Haverty
Family Foundation
and
The William T. Kemper Foundation –
Commerce Bank, Trustee

Kansas City's
UNION STATION
Reflections After 100 Years

By Roy Inman; chapter introductions by Kevin Murphy
Edited by Doug Weaver
Designed by David Spaw
Copy-edited by Diane McLendon

Published by Kansas City Star Books
1729 Grand Blvd.
Kansas City, Missouri 64108

All rights reserved.
Copyright © 2014 by Roy Inman and The Kansas City Star

No part of this book may be reproduced, stored in a retrieval system, or transmitted in any form or by any means electronic, mechanical, photocopying, recording or otherwise, without the prior consent of the publisher. Unless otherwise credited in the caption, all photographs are by Roy Inman.

First edition, first printing
ISBN: 978-1-61169-142-9
Library of Congress Control Number: 2014948289

Printed in the United States.

To order copies, call 816-234-4292.

TABLE OF CONTENTS

Chapter 1
The Glory Years 3

Chapter 2
The Decline 12

Chapter 3
The Demolition And The Restoration 34

Chapter 4
The Station's Rebirth 64

Chapter 5
The Future of Union Station 88

ACKNOWLEDGEMENTS

A project of this scope and spanning two decades owes much to many.
I cannot begin to thank all who contributed, but YOU know who you are ☺

There are particular people to whom I wish to send a thousand "thank yous!":

Andy Scott, who gave me the opportunity to document the restoration of
Kansas City's most cherished landmark.

George Guastello and his team, who
a) saved the station so that it now has a future and
b) allowed and encouraged me to continue photographing.

Mike Haverty and **Jonathan Kemper.**
Through their generous support, this book became a physical reality.

George Inman, my first assistant on the long project.

Lloyd Dillinger, whose knowledge of the station helped in immeasurable ways.

Jim Asplund was my go-to guy for solid information about Union Station and all things train.

Pete and **Carolyn McMasters,** who archived the tens of thousands of prints from my Union Station
documentation. May they rest in peace.

Kathy Wismer, assistant. • **Bob Agne,** assistant. • **Chris Dahquist,** assistant.

Much of the research for the editorial content by **Kevin Murphy** came from a previous Union Station book, "Union Station:
Kansas City," by **Jeffrey Spivak.** It was also published by Kansas City Star Books.

And of course, a huge thank you and a hug to my dear wife, **Barbara,** who put up with my long days, nights and weekends
away from home when I was working on the station photography.

-Roy Inman

Foreword

*by Michael R. Haverty,
Former chairman of Union Station Kansas City, Inc.*

Roy Inman has wanted to do this book for a long time. In 2008, he visited with Commerce Bank's Jonathan Kemper and me to see if we might support the project. We both liked the idea, but times were tough at Union Station and in the economy back then. This book needed to be a celebration, and we resolved that we'd go ahead with the project in better times. The station's centennial certainly qualifies.

We've known Roy and admired his photography for years, and we understood that he had taken more than 50,000 pictures in 1996-1999, documenting Union Station's restoration. It was an extraordinary commitment, done with no thought of monetary reward. Roy simply loved the building and wanted to share its story.

Jonathan and I feel the same way, for slightly different but overlapping reasons. Jonathan has a strong personal interest in architectural preservation, including serving as chairman of the National Trust for Historic Places. He also served on the Station's Preservation Advisory Committee, which helped oversee the Station's restoration. The William T. Kemper Foundation, with Jonathan as its co-trustee, was a major donor to the Station's restoration fund-raising campaign.

Jonathan cares a lot about the collection of streets, parks and buildings that define a city. In many ways, Union Station has been a defining building for Kansas City. It marked the city's coming of age from a bustling frontier town to a modern city of refinement and culture. When it opened in 1914, local residents believed that Kansas City had arrived, and they believed that travelers would feel the same way. Now, 100 years later, Union Station has become the defining building for Kansas City and a point of pride for its residents.

Michael R. Haverty

But there's another reason why Jonathan and I love this building. We're both into history, and in this town, history often gets back to railroads. Kansas City wouldn't be the same if the Hannibal & St. Joseph Railroad hadn't chosen this place to build the first bridge across the Missouri River in 1869. And it was the railroads that built Union Station – 12 of them that came together to create a magnificent structure designed by architect Jarvis Hunt to provide a true transportation center of the United States.

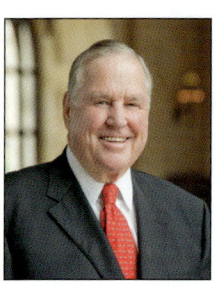

I've been associated with three of those railroads in my career – Missouri Pacific; Atchison, Topeka & Santa Fe; and Kansas City Southern – but my ties to Union Station go back to my childhood in the 1950s. I'm a fourth-generation railroader: My great-grandfather came from Ireland and settled in Atchison, and his son and grandson (my dad) were railroaders before me. When I was a kid, I used to travel on Dad's pass, along with my brother Joe and my grandmother Myrtle Pruslow. We went all over the country, but our travels began and ended at Union Station. I gained an appreciation for the epoch of this country's settlement and for the part the railroads played in it – and, when I returned home, I understood what a great city and station we have here.

Many metropolitan Kansas Citians also loved the station, and that's why voters on both sides of the state line approved a sales tax in 1996 to restore it. The reborn building was even better than any of us remembered, and there's no doubt that saving it was the right thing to do. The station started a renaissance in the surrounding area. The Postal Service moved into the station, and the IRS redeveloped the old Post Office site. The National Archives and the Kansas City Ballet moved into newly-restored, historical buildings on station property, and the Federal Reserve Bank was drawn to the neighborhood, too. Old warehouses in the Crossroads District became loft apartments, and the arts and dining scene also got new life. Unfortunately, the station's initial business model proved to be erroneous, and within a few years, Union Station was fighting to keep the doors open.

The station's darkest time was probably 2005, and in that year, I inherited the board chairman position of Union Station Kansas City, Inc. It took painful cuts and a revised business model, but things began to turn around a few years later. Several civic organizations now call the station home, including the Greater Kansas City Chamber of Commerce, the Kansas City Area Development Council and the Kansas City Board of Elections. Union Station has been profitable for the past several years under the leadership of CEO George Guastello, and it's expected to remain so. USKC, Inc. is a private corporation, and it doesn't receive any taxpayer funding.

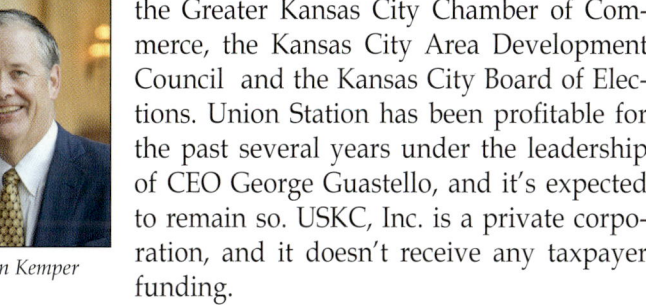

Jonathan Kemper

Roy Inman will take you through this history in the gorgeous photos that follow. The story opens with a look at the glory years and the years of decline. Then glimpse what only Roy and the construction crews saw: the loving attention to detail that brought the station back to life and prepared it for its modern role. Happy birthday, Union Station!

A Colorful Lineup – *Artist Anthony Benton Gude used locomotives to represent the 12 railroads that financed the construction of Kansas City's Union Station. They were, from left: Chicago Great Western, Rock Island, Union Pacific, Missouri-Kansas-Texas, Missouri Pacific, Santa Fe, Kansas City Southern, Frisco, Wabash, Burlington, Chicago & Alton and Milwaukee Road. Station architect Jarvis Hunt's likeness floats in the exhaust from the Chicago & Alton locomotive. Also see pgs. 46/47*

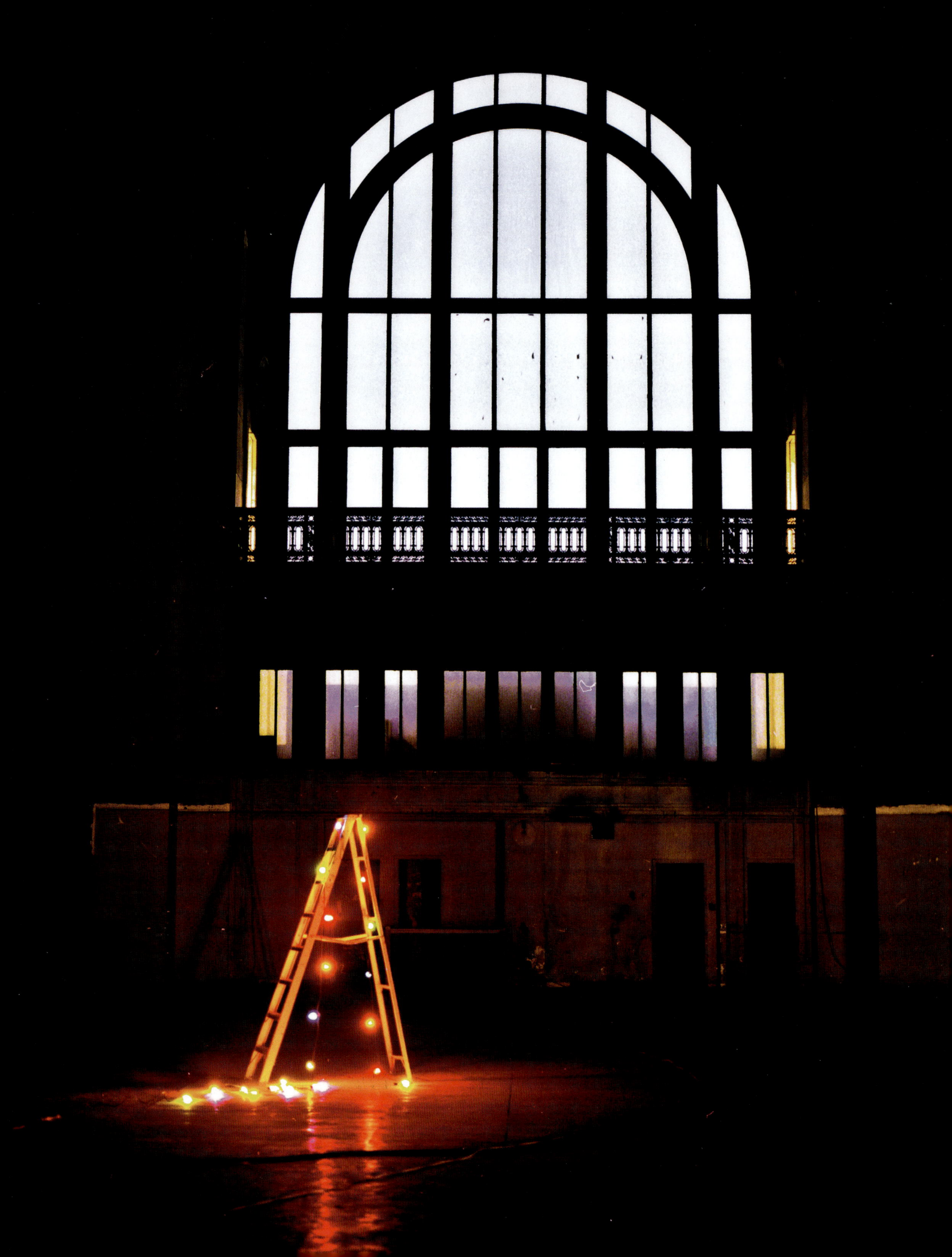

Union Station
Introduction

When Andy Scott asked if I would be interested in shooting the restoration of Union Station, I immediately realized that it was a once-in-a-lifetime opportunity.

I knew it would be the largest photography project I would ever undertake. What I did not realize was that it would also be a life-changing one. Not only did I spend thousands of hours doing the actual photography, I also experienced an epiphany that made me understand the overriding significance of the station to Kansas City, to the region, to America, and by extrapolation, to the world. Railroads were at the center of the industrial revolution, and the most visible artifacts from that time of trains are the remaining Great Stations of the 19th and early-20th centuries. Union Station is one of those grand rail terminals.

Roy Inman on the job at the station, 1998. Photo by Charlie Brenneke.

The photography went on long after the restoration phase from 1994 to 1999. Some construction work continued for a few months afterward, and as you will see, many new attractions and businesses have been added. I never stopped taking pictures, and I still contribute images to the collection.

I had one overriding objective in doing this book: I wanted others to see what I saw and photographed. In some situations, my assistants and I were the only humans there, on the ground, during the amazing transformation. At other times, some workers were present. This book is for the legions of Union Station fans, and also for those who helped pay for the restoration with their 1/8th cent sales tax contribution. They deserve a more intimate look at one of America's greatest restoration projects. I figure if you pay, you ought to get to play, so to speak.

It was difficult to edit 50,000 images down to the couple of hundred in these pages. As my grandson Jacob Krafft and I pored over book after book of prints, boxes of negatives and thousands of slides and transparencies, the memories of those magical, nostalgic times engulfed me, like standing outside the station on a misty night, enveloped by a comforting fog.

There were rickety ladders and rooms so darkly ominous that I could barely force myself to walk into them. There were days so cold that extension cords rebelled at being rolled up. There were spooky nights when we were sure we weren't alone. There was the 85'+ tall Grand Hall scaffolding with its 119 steps; heavy cameras, lights, stands, tripods and cords were strapped on painful shoulders as we trudged to the top. And I would do it all again.

Perhaps the most astute observation came from a conversation I had with Julian Davis, aka "Chewy." He was one of the men responsible for the recreation of the station's ceilings. He told me about other jobs that he and his Hayles and Howe compatriots had worked on, mentioning The White House and Buckingham Palace, among others.

I said those were some pretty high-profile structures.

"Yes," he replied, but emphatically added, "Roy, Union Station is Kansas City's castle."

- Roy Inman

George and Lloyd, Above – *The two guys who spent the most time helping with the photography of the restoration were George Inman, left, and Lloyd Dillinger.*

Christmas Ladder, Left – *It wasn't all blood, sweat, tears and toil. There were lighter moments, such as when we worked during Christmas week. We thought that strings of holiday lights might brighten the gloom of the dark, cold station.*

CHAPTER 1
THE GLORY YEARS

Any telling of Kansas City history can't overlook Union Station.

The immense structure – two blocks wide and fronted by six towering stone columns – was born as a transportation hub, evolved into a social center, endured a painful decline and prolonged closure and then returned to vigorous life as a nexus for business and culture.

Union Station opened on Oct. 30, 1914, to a booming salute of canons as an estimated 100,000 people celebrated the city's stunning new landmark. Inside, thousands of people crowded the Grand Hall to gaze at its elaborate 95-foot-high ceiling and soaring archway windows, flooded in sunlight.

The Kansas City Journal said the new station was a milestone in the development of Kansas City. "It marks the closing of one era and the opening of another," said the paper on the day of the opening.

Civic leaders and railroad companies had talked for years about the need for a new train station. At the turn of the century, Kansas City was a raucous river town, a gateway to the Western frontier and a booming crossroads of rail traffic. But the demand for trains out of Kansas City overwhelmed the capacity of Union Depot, a West Bottoms station that was cramped, dirty and prone to flooding.

After years of negotiations, civic and private entities and the railroads agreed on a new depot at 23rd Street and Grand Avenue. The 12 railroad lines worked together as a "union" for the project, thus the name Union Station.

The station would require public approval because the city had to grant rights-of-way for construction of some rail bridges over city streets. The vote in 1909 was overwhelmingly favorable – 24,522 to 708.

The search for someone to design Union Station led to Jarvis Hunt, a prominent Chicago architect who designed homes for wealthy businessmen and had spent several years drawing up plans for the new station. He was given a simple instruction: "Make a monument."

Construction began in 1910. The work was grueling as men

Continued on page 5

Steam and Snow – *Charlie Brenneke took this classic steam and snow photograph, shot looking west from the Penn Street Bridge, on Feb. 13, 1948. During the restoration, the bridge was rebuilt as a ramp to the Union Station parking lot. An inbound Rock Island steamer with its passenger cars was changing tracks to align with the proper gate. The two workers had probably just cleared snow and ice from one of the switches, a necessary and continuous task on railroads during the winter.*

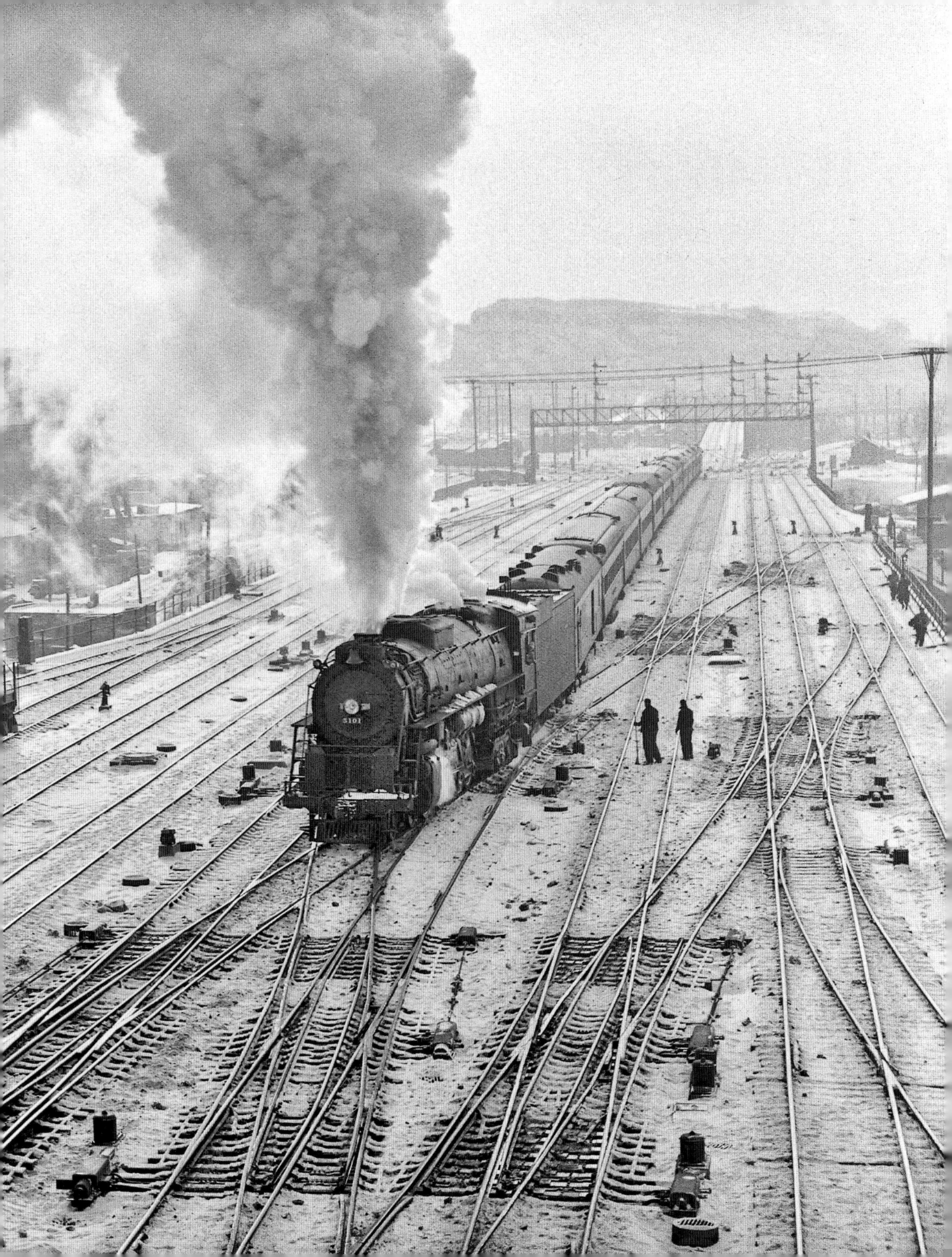
5101

4   KANSAS CITY'S UNION STATION

Continued from page 2

dug, drilled and blasted away soil and rock and hoisted massive amounts of steel, concrete and limestone for the building. Five men died during construction, which was also marred by labor disputes and job site walk-offs.

But by the time of the grand opening, Union Station was a citywide source of pride, a landmark in the making. Its ultimate cost, including land, adjacent buildings and new train yards, reached $48 million. The station included 105,000 square feet of marble floors. The Grand Hall was more than 200 feet wide and the North Waiting Room was 350 feet long.

While some chided the building as too extravagant, "The Architectural Record" called it "consistent, dignified, sufficiently monumental and massive to be worthy of a great city."

In its early years, Union Station not only served tens of thousands of rail passengers but also became a place to be seen. People went to ogle the building's grandeur, to dine, spoon ice cream sodas and browse its many shops for books, toys, food and other sundries. At Christmas, the station was adorned for the season, and children would wait in long lines to see Santa. Many festive New Years' Eves were celebrated under the big clock.

Union Station became a stopover for presidents and famous celebrities, such as Clark Gable, Jimmy Durante, Douglas Fairbanks, Jr. and Jack Dempsey.

Perhaps nothing besides trains became more synonymous with Union Station than the Fred Harvey lunchroom, where waitresses in identical white smocks were known as the Harvey Girls. The women, required to be single, attractive, of good character and between the ages of 18 and 30, waited on customers around a horseshoe-shaped counter and surrounding tables.

While Union Station bustled, the outside world was start-

Copy continued on page 6

1912, Top Left – *Union Station was almost exactly two years from completion when this photo was taken on Oct. 1, 1912. The classic arch windows have yet to be completed and the roof has not been installed. Photographer unknown.*

Mid '50s, Top Middle – *In 1956, Union Station was still a busy transportation hub, although passenger rail traffic had decreased dramatically since World War II. The 800-foot-long train sheds were still in place and more than a dozen taxicabs were triple-parked awaiting fares.*

Misplaced Moon, Top Right – *There is an intriguing anomaly to this photograph, probably from the late 1950s. The clouds are apparently backlit by the moon. But the moon never appears over Union Station in that part of the sky. Consensus is that a commonly used, tedious darkroom technique accomplished this contradiction. It was called "double printing" and involved making one exposure of the main image on the photographic paper, removing that negative from the enlarger and inserting another negative with another image, in this case, the moon. Photographer unknown.*

Train Sheds, Bottom Left – *This aerial view of Union Station and surrounds shows how the rail center was laid out. Sheds nearly 800 feet long extended from the east and west sides and protected passengers from the elements. Date is unknown, but judging by the finished United States Post Office building at the bottom left and the as-yet-to-be developed Signboard Hill, the photo was probably taken in the 1950s. Photographer unknown.*

Vintage New Year's Eve, Above – *Right at the stroke of midnight in an unknown year, the photographer (name also unknown) popped the flashbulb and recorded part of the huge crowd that typically descended on Union Station to ring in the New Year. The top of the ticketing counter is visible in the far right corner of the photograph.*

The Harvey Girls, Right – *Fred Harvey's food and service were legendary onboard Santa Fe dining cars, as well as in his restaurants inside depots along the railroad's route. The Harvey Girls, as his waitresses were known, were efficient, mild mannered and wore starched-white, nun-like uniforms. They were also the inspiration of a 1946 movie starring Judy Garland, "The Harvey Girls." Harvey's employment standards were high and not very politically correct by today's standards. He advertised for "single young women, 18 to 30 years of age, of good character, attractive and intelligent." Photographer unknown.*

Up The Escalators, Middle Right – *Escalators carried passengers and the ever-present, ever-friendly Red Caps to and from track level. This photo shows the Station Master and probably another station official. A photographer with Anderson Studio captured the scene.*

Flooded Depot, Far Bottom Right – *The old Union Depot in the West Bottoms flooded with regularity, bringing train traffic to a standstill. Leaders of the rapidly-growing Kansas City could not tolerate this disruption in rail travel. A new, far larger Union Station was envisioned up the hill. This photo was probably taken inside the Union Depot. Note the high water mark indication from a June 1, 1903 flood. Photographer unknown.*

THE GLORY YEARS   9

Holiday Station, Left – *This angle from the north end of the North Waiting Room is not a typical view shown in photographs from earlier eras. The date and photographer are unknown, but the long benches were in place, a convenience booth centered the room, and the station was decorated for the holidays.*

The Traveler's Aid, Below – *The Traveler's Aid Society is an organization whose roots go back to the 19th century. It was started in St. Louis to help travelers heading west, and in the following decades, the concept had spread to cities across America, including Kansas City and Union Station. Four-year-old Betty Neely posed on the counter as a promotion for the Society in this photo by Cressway Studios.*

Continued from page 6

enough employees to carry and load bags or to sort and handle heavy volumes of mail in the station's basement. Women stepped up to take jobs traditionally held by men – driving baggage carts, loading and unloading boxcars and working the passenger ticket counters.

When the war finally ended in 1945, Union Station was the scene of joyous homecomings as soldiers returned to their loved ones. But the war's end also marked a turning point for Union Station. Inevitable declines in rail passenger numbers lay ahead and so did an exodus of Kansas City residents to the suburbs, making Union Station less present in their lives. The venerable station was in for a prolonged challenge.

Tale of a Master, Right – *Frank Meister was a very talented amateur photographer who dramatically chronicled in stunning black and white images his hometown of Kansas City. One of his favorite subjects was Union Station, and his photograph of Grand Hall, c. 1950, was an instant classic. Meister's work was exhibited on five continents, and he was a member of the Royal Photographic Society of London, one of only 150 non-Brits to be elected to that exclusive club. He never had a family of his own. Ruth, the woman of his dreams, rejected his proposal of marriage because her parents felt that a mere teller at the First National Bank (his day job) did not have prospects. At some time late in his life, frustrated at not receiving the recognition he felt he deserved in his hometown and his marriage proposal rejected, he burned all of his negatives, so there was no prime source for his images. He died at age 91. Roy Inman copied this photograph with a large format view camera from a print that still hung on the wall in the building previously occupied by First National Bank, which had at that time become American National Bank.*

Traveler from 1938, Below – *Bags weighing him down, a traveler looking already weary, makes his way down the 350-foot length of the North Waiting Room in this 1938 photograph by Charlie Brenneke. Not only was Union Station where people got on and off a train, it was Kansas City's gathering place, especially on New Year's Eve and other holidays. It was also a place where anyone with the wherewithal could dine in style at Fred Harvey's or purchase something for the kids from House of Toys (at right), considered at the time to be one of the premier shops of its kind in the city.*

12

Chapter 2
The Decline

The year was 1946, and Union Station once again became a place where travel meant seeing family and friends instead of sending young men to war. The mood in the station was buoyant, as the Grand Hall hummed with travelers, shoppers and diners.

While train traffic was naturally not as high as during the war, in 1947 there were more riders than in any year since 1930. The station looked splendid, too, as ceilings were washed for the first time, restoring colors that decades of cigarette smoke had obscured. And the station finally got escalators, which shuttled passengers between the main floor and track levels below.

Nationally, railroad companies took a new approach to rail travel as they introduced some 250 diesel-powered streamliners in 1948 with just 100 passenger seats instead of 500. The new trains were more efficient and arrived at their destinations sooner. Some new trains had elevated, glass-encased observation cars for panoramic viewing. Among the new trains were the Santa Fe Railroad's Kansas City Chief and Burlington's Zephyr, two lines that became service hallmarks for decades.

The nimble new streamliners were profitable at the outset but could not overcome a steady shift from rail travel in America. Passenger numbers nationally fell to less than 800 million in 1946, down from nearly 1 billion during the height of the war that ended in 1945. By 1949, ridership dropped to less than 600 million, and in 1957 to less than 400 million. Cars and commercial airlines were drawing people from the slower pace of trains. A plane could get someone from Kansas City to Chicago in about an hour; a train would take all day.

At Union Station, rail traffic in the 25 years after the war dropped from 1.1 million in 1945 to just more than 54,000 in 1971. By the late 1950s, some railroads eliminated passenger service, and even some companies pulled out of Kansas City entirely.

Union Station was growing ever-more empty and looking outdated. In 1957-58, the station interior got a facelift, including Fred Harvey's. The lunch counter and stools were removed in favor of a futuristic-looking cocktail lounge. A neon sign went up over the east entrance of the restaurant, and tile was laid over the marble floor. Glass walls were built around the candy store and bookstore

Continued on page 14

Water Everywhere – *It was sad to see that the once magnificent North Waiting Room of Union Station had come to such a pass. The ceiling was literally falling down in chunks. After even a brief rain, water accumulated in puddles on the floor, two inches deep in some places. This was the first photograph Roy Inman took in 1995 at the start of his five-year-long documentation of the restoration.*

Round And Round, Above & Top Right – *The Circle Theatre was the first resident equity playhouse in Kansas City. The company performed in the round in what was once the Immigrants Waiting Room at the end of the North Waiting Room and staged 42 productions during the life of the theatrical operation, 1962-1967. The Bacchus charitable organization picked The Circle Theatre as the recipient of its fundraiser in 1966 and promoted the event with style.*

Continued from page 13

and at the restaurant entrance. The idea was to make the station look more modern, but the contrast to the rest of the grand old architecture was stark.

As passenger traffic dwindled, railroad companies clung to cargo and mail service to stay in business, but in 1967, the postal service stopped using mail cars on trains. Union Station couldn't even keep Fred Harvey's, which was sold to a national company that closed its railroad cafes to focus on airport and roadside locations.

In 1971, Amtrak took over rail service at Union Station and cut more routes. Passengers were served on just five or six routes a day, in dirty, unkempt cars. The waiting room was closed, and passengers waited on plastic bucket chairs in Grand Hall.

Union Station still hosted periodic galas, including the Baccus Ball in the spring of 1972. Later that year, the station would see its last big event when Democratic presidential candidate George

McGovern drew some 25,000 people for a speech a month before losing the election.

As the station continued its slow demise, in the background people debated how to save it. A Chicago consultant, hired by station operator Terminal Railway, proposed tearing down the station and replacing it with apartments and an office high-rise building. The consultant said the operating costs of Union Station were no longer justified.

The community recoiled. Demolish Union Station? It may have been past its prime, but civic and corporate leaders and a sentimental public wouldn't hear of the building being torn down. Thus began many years of Kansas City asking the question: "What should we do with Union Station?"

In February 1972, the local Landmarks Commission succeeded in getting the station added to the National Register of Historic Places, which made its destruction harder to achieve. Mayor

Continued on page 17

Past Thespians – *The blonde brick walls just inside the theatre entrance were covered with the signatures of actors and the plays in which they performed.*

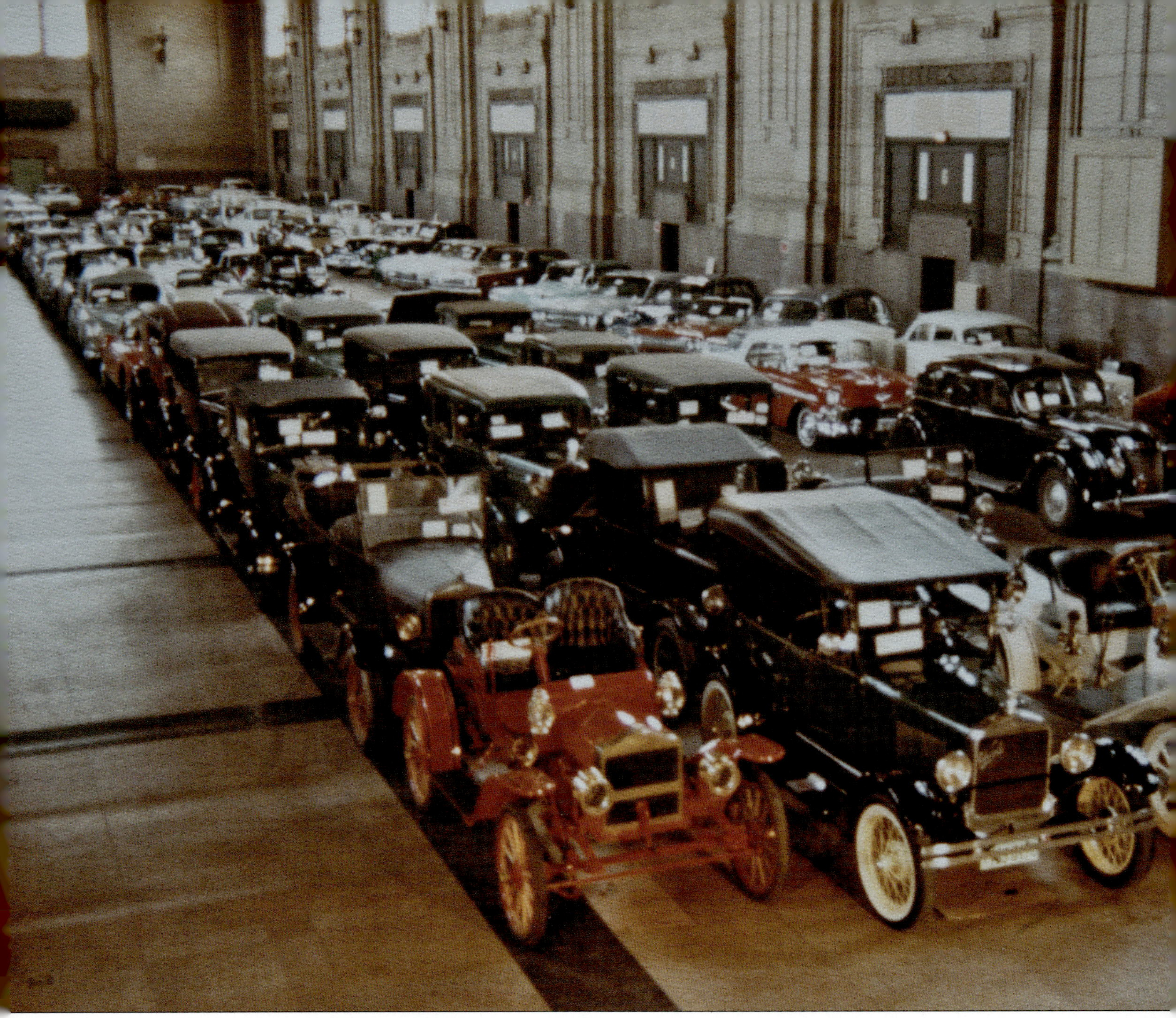

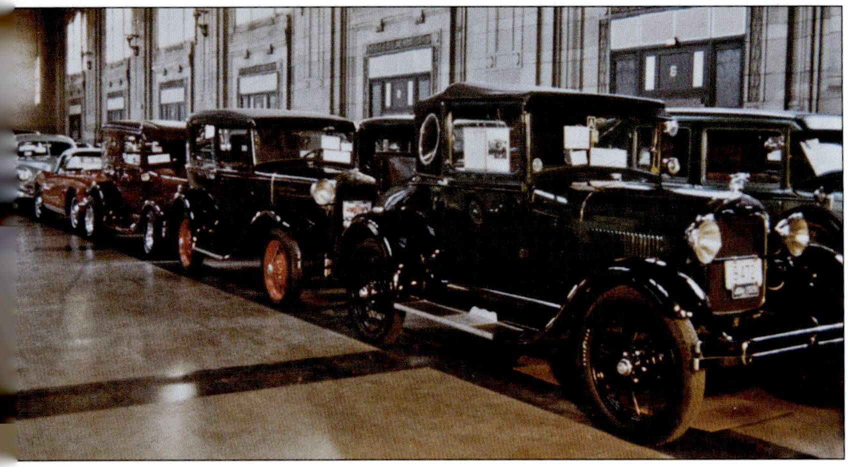

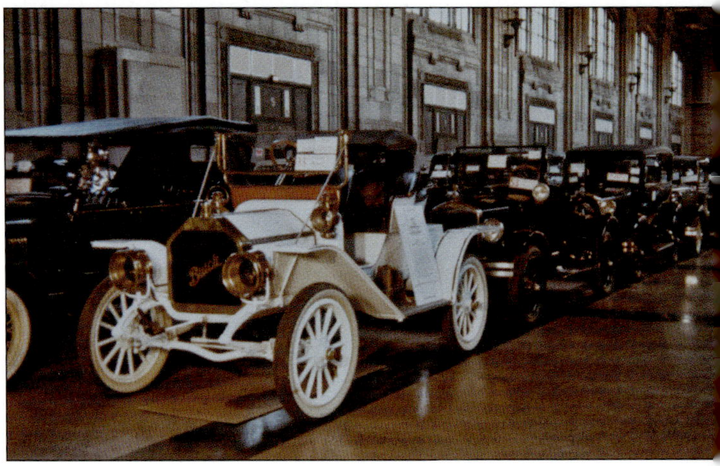

THE DECLINE 17

Continued from page 15

Charles Wheeler appointed a city commission to suggest suitable and affordable uses for the building.

In July 1974, Missouri Gov. Kit Bond headlined a meeting of more than 300 business and political leaders to discuss ways to save Union Station. A large Canadian real estate firm called Trizec Corp. Ltd. agreed to create a redevelopment plan for the station that called for converting it into a shopping center, surrounded by new hotels, high-rise apartments, town homes and a science museum. Although the developer had no tenants signed up for the site, the Kansas City Council gave the plan a thumbs-up.

Union Station was in for a new life, but it had to dispense with the clutter in order to make room. On two days in June 1975, thousands of items in the station went up for public auction. Just about everything was for sale – desks, chairs, bunk beds, waiting benches, cabinets, brass wall clocks, old cash registers, typewriters, Fred Harvey uniforms, bar stools, even slabs of marble.

"You'll be buying a piece of history," auctioneer Jerry Herzog told the crowds. And so they did. Union Station was emptied, leaving a hollow ring inside the station that would last for many years.

Continued on page 23

Old Wheels – *Shanks Auto Display, also known as Shanks Auto Museum, occupied most of the North Waiting Room from about 1975 to 1984, when the lease was terminated due to the imminent closing of the station. Jim and Nina Shanks were the owners/operators and greeted guests and buyers from all over America and from many foreign countries. At any one time, there were 140 cars lined up in neat rows running the 350-foot length of the huge room. At first, the cars were from Jim and Nina's own collection and from those of friends, but soon they were accepting autos from a wide range of owners. Jim ran a successful construction business, and Nina was on the ground at the station working in the museum. Very shortly, they began to charge auto owners a $25 storage fee and took a 10 percent commission fee when a car sold. There was also a $1.50 general admission fee. Grandson Jim Shanks ("None of us is a 'jr.' or 'II' because we all have different middle names.") has mementoes and artifacts from the museum, including the original "Shanks Auto Display Open 7 Days A Week" sign that he is holding. Photo at bottom right shows Jim and Nina at the display in Union Station. Photos from grandson Jim Shanks' collection.*

Inside the building, Top – *A fine layer of gray dust blanketed every horizontal surface, giving the interior a ghostly appearance. This ornate stair railing has been restored and leads to the lower level of Pierpont's Restaurant.*

Days Gone By, Above – *Weeds and native prairie grasses had taken over the grounds around the station by 1995. Closed and abandoned for a decade, only hints of its role as one of America's greatest rail terminals remained, such as a few railroad logos on some interior doors, rusty rails and disintegrating ties. The camera looks southeast in this photo that was one of a series Roy Inman shot for the archives of the National Register of Historic Places.*

The Iconic Santa Fe, Right – *The w ar bonnet livery was still being cared for in 1972, a year after Amtrak took over passenger service on most American railroads. The train sheds were rusting away, and passenger traffic was down to a trickle. Photograph by Charlie Brenneke.*

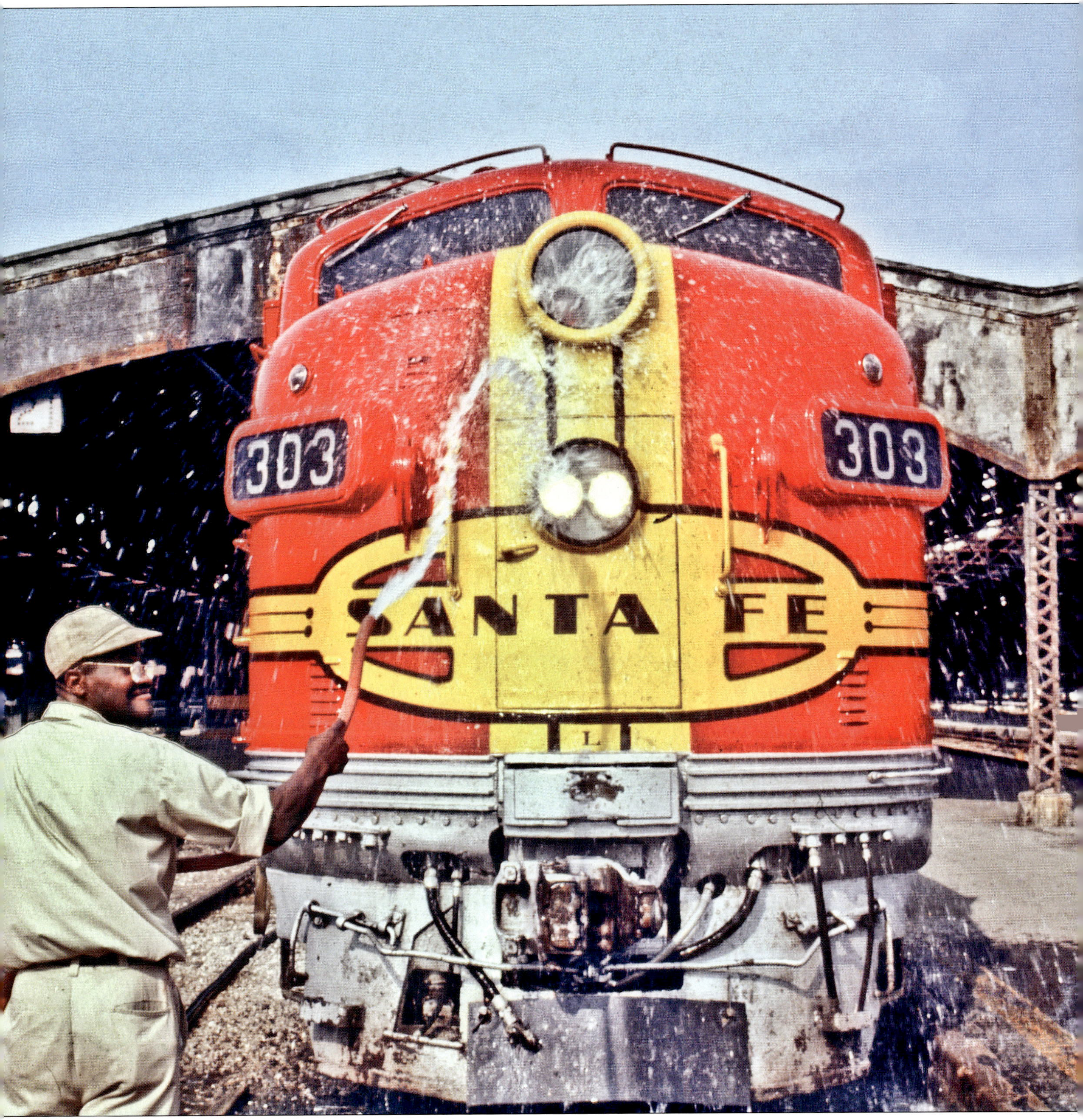
303
303
SANTA FE

Grimy, Top – Baggage and freight carts kept things moving between trains and the station for decades. They had carried tons of suitcases and shipped items. By the late 1990s, they were parked at the far end of the 60,000-square-foot basement, or C level, their wood rotting and stakes rusting.

Peeling Paint, Above – The broken glass along the east canopy, rusting metal framing and supports, all signs that Union Station was rapidly going downhill and if not rescued very soon, it would be too late.

Workbench Clutter, Right – And you think YOUR workbench is cluttered! This vignette was typical of what greeted workers when restoration began in 1995. Everything was either rusty, dirty or dusty in the extreme, toxic or all of the above. Such is the stuff of which gritty photos are made.

THE DECLINE 21

22 Kansas City's Union Station

Continued from page 17

Like much of Kansas City, Union Station took a hard blow in September 1977 as historic rainfall overflowed creeks and roads and filled many a basement with water. Rain pelted the aging, leaky Union Station roof, already damaged from previous rains. Flakes of the ornate ceiling crashed to the floor.

Trizec continued to look for someone to occupy Union Station and the proposed new buildings under its grand redevelopment scheme. A second business, Pershing Square Redevelopment Corp., was created as a shell corporation to seek development tax breaks from the state of Missouri.

Well into the 1980s, there was still nothing serious in the offing for Trizec, as Union Station sat mostly empty. The costs of heat and power in the building mounted until the heat was turned off and Amtrak passengers waited for trains in a polyester bubble set up in the Grand Hall.

Angry and impatient, city leaders in 1988 hired lawyers to pursue legal action against Trizec and Pershing Square Redevelopment for not making good on the redevelopment plan. For four years, under the glare of the media and public, the city and Trizec sparred over what would be a fair settlement, with the city wanting $91 million in damages. Trizec offered less than $20 million. In the end,

Continued on page 28

Worn Out, Left – *The classic carriage pavilion on the west side of Union Station was badly deteriorated in 1995. At first examination, engineers thought that some of the canopy could be saved. But when the demolition began, they realized that it was a total loss and had to be completely reconstructed.*

No Sheds, Below – *A late December 1974 photograph by Charlie Brenneke shows what the once-bustling train station had become. A glowing, setting sun does little to enhance the grim, gray mood. The 800-foot-long train sheds were gone, along with most of the passengers they once protected from rain and snow. On this day, a single, tarnished passenger observation car at the end of a westbound train was the only rail traffic.*

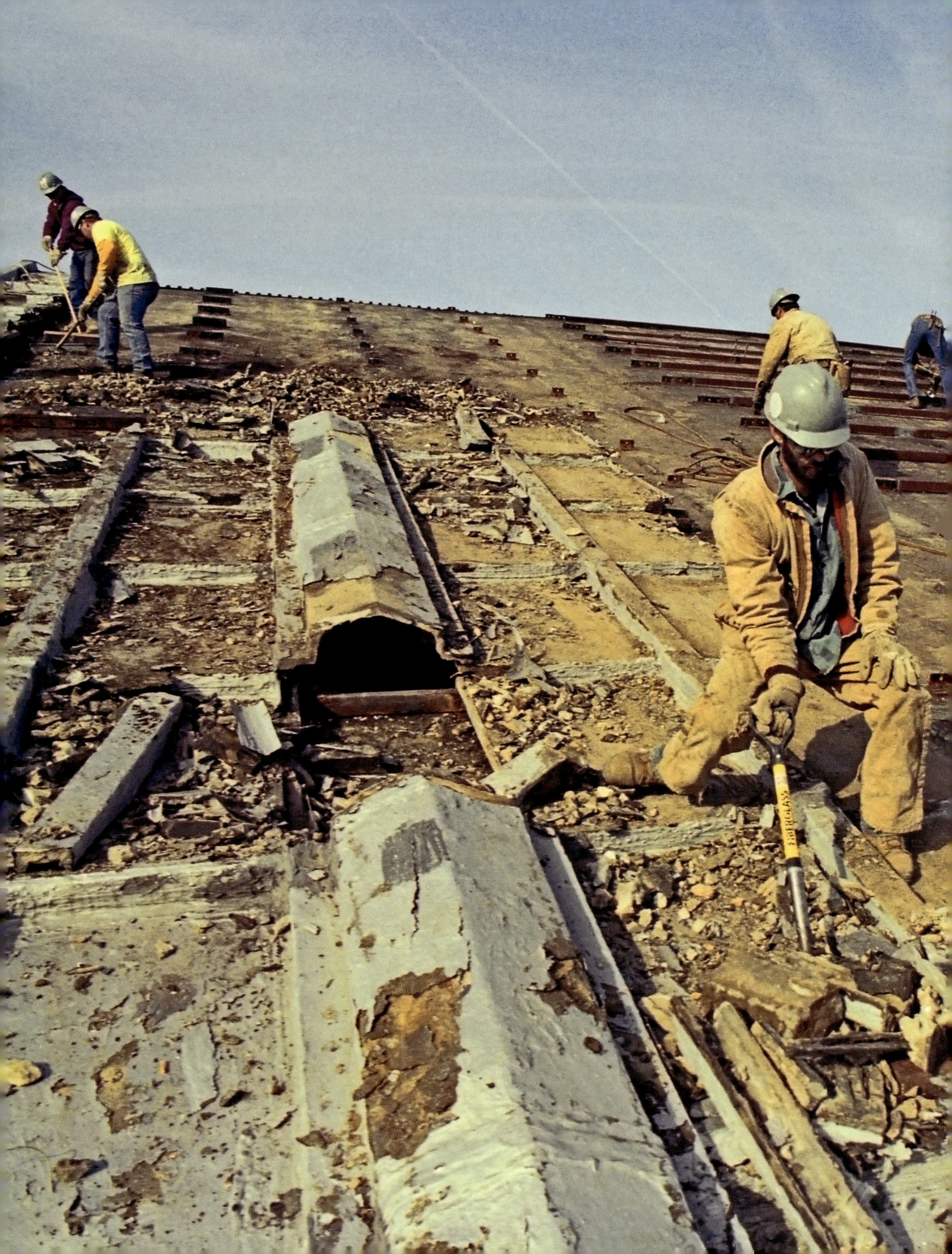

THE DECLINE   25

Getting To The Bottom Of It – *The old roof above the Grand Hall was demolished down to the bare bones. It was heavy, dirty, labor-intensive work on a steep incline. The photo above shows that initial phase. The photo at left shows more of the demo work, plus the next two steps in the process in the background.*

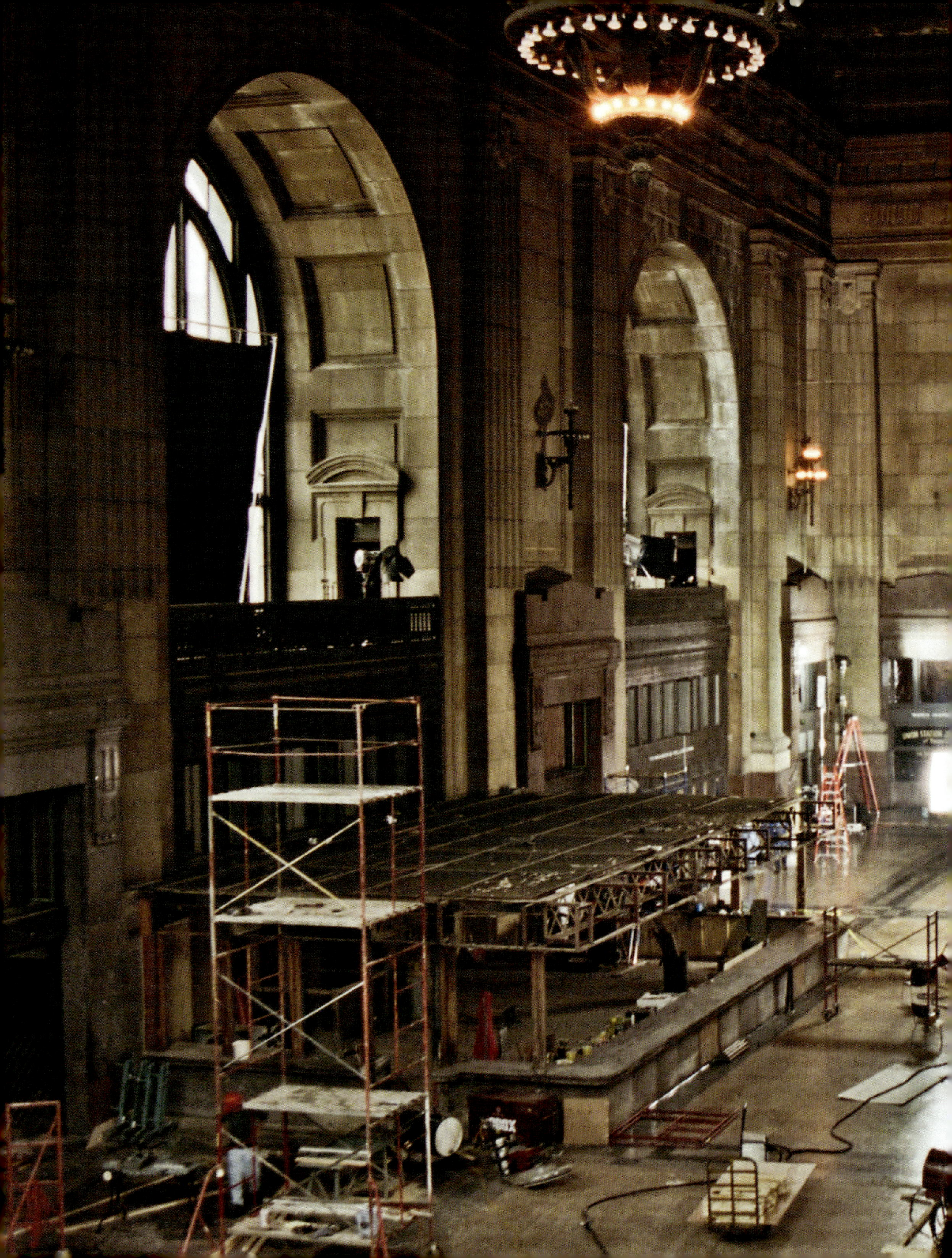

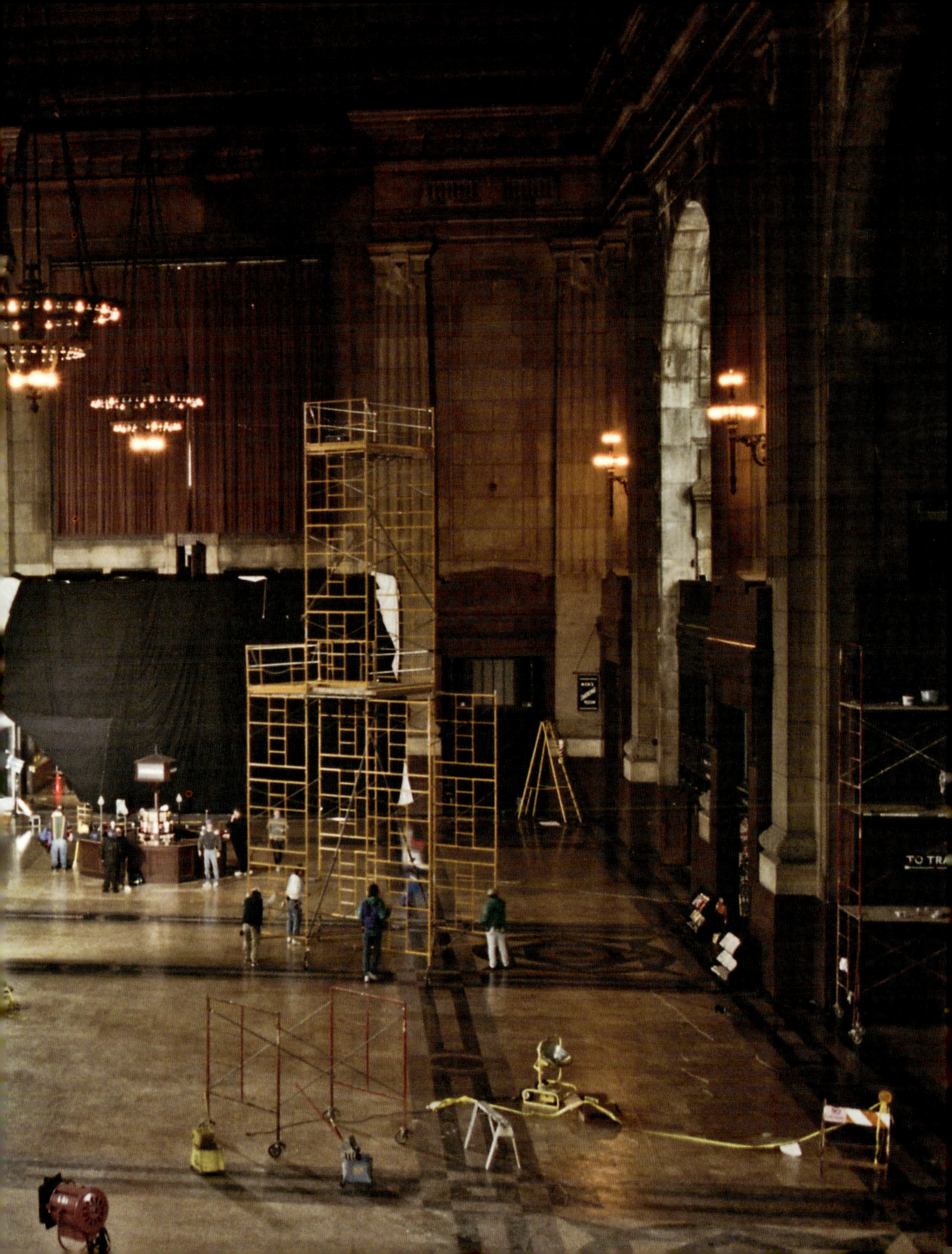

Continued from page 23

Trizec paid $1.5 million and gave ownership of the station to a non-profit group, Union Station Assistance Corp. That was 1994, but the future of the station remained unknown.

To survive, Union Station needed money. Executives from some major Kansas City corporations, including Sprint and Hallmark, set out to raise half the estimated $100 million cost of renovating the decaying station. The rest would need to come from taxpayers. Some money was lined up from federal grants, but local taxes would be required to pay for renovation and operation of the building.

The editorial pages of The Kansas City Star floated the idea of a sales tax – not just in Kansas City but in Johnson and Wyandotte counties in Kansas and Platte and Clay counties in Missouri. It was an unlikely marriage that crossed state lines and became known as the bi-state tax, which required preliminary approval of legislatures in Missouri and Kansas.

The tax would be one-quarter cent and pay for station renovation

Continued on page 33

History Made Live – *Hollywood came to Kansas City just before the restoration began in earnest, and two major motion pictures included scenes that were shot at Union Station. The late director Robert Altman used massive light-modifiers in the Grand Hall, pages 24/25, to create the dark, brooding mood he was after in his film "Kansas City." The HBO documentary "Truman" (the four photographs on this page) was based on David McCullough's Pulitzer Prize-winning book of the same name. Partially shot in and around Union Station in 1995, the movie starred Gary Sinise as President Harry S. Truman (waving to the crowd) and Diana Scarwid as Bess Wallace Truman (at his side). The film aired in September of 1995. Hundreds of extras were dressed in 1950s clothes for the big welcoming home scene in the North Waiting Room. Historic details were added, including benches and train announcement boards next to each gate. The movie crew, some with the cryptic "'Truman': Bullet-Proof Grips" printed on their shirts, worked outside to create a dusk scene around the old car. The film earned several honors, including one for Gary Sinise, who won the Golden Globe Best Actor award In A Made For TV Movie.*

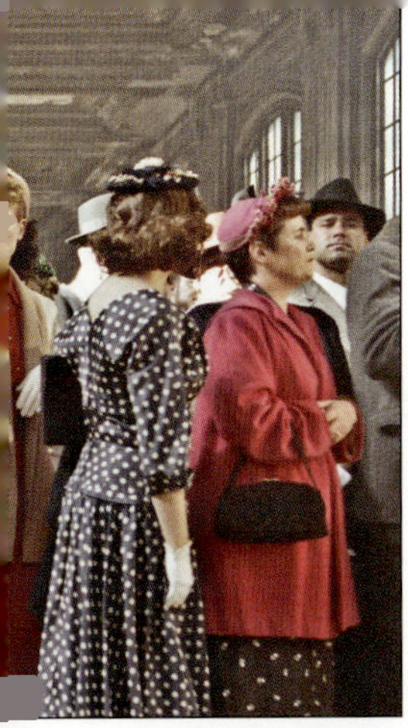

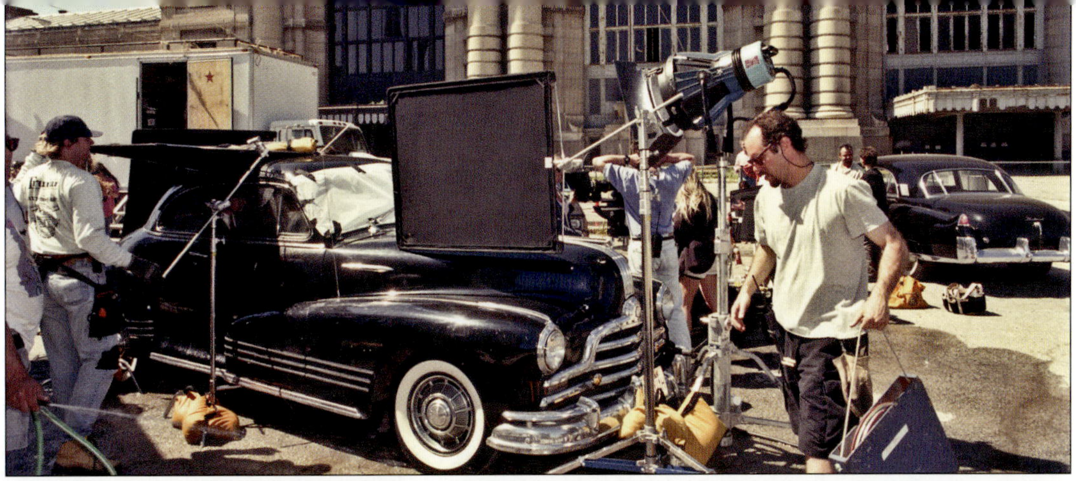

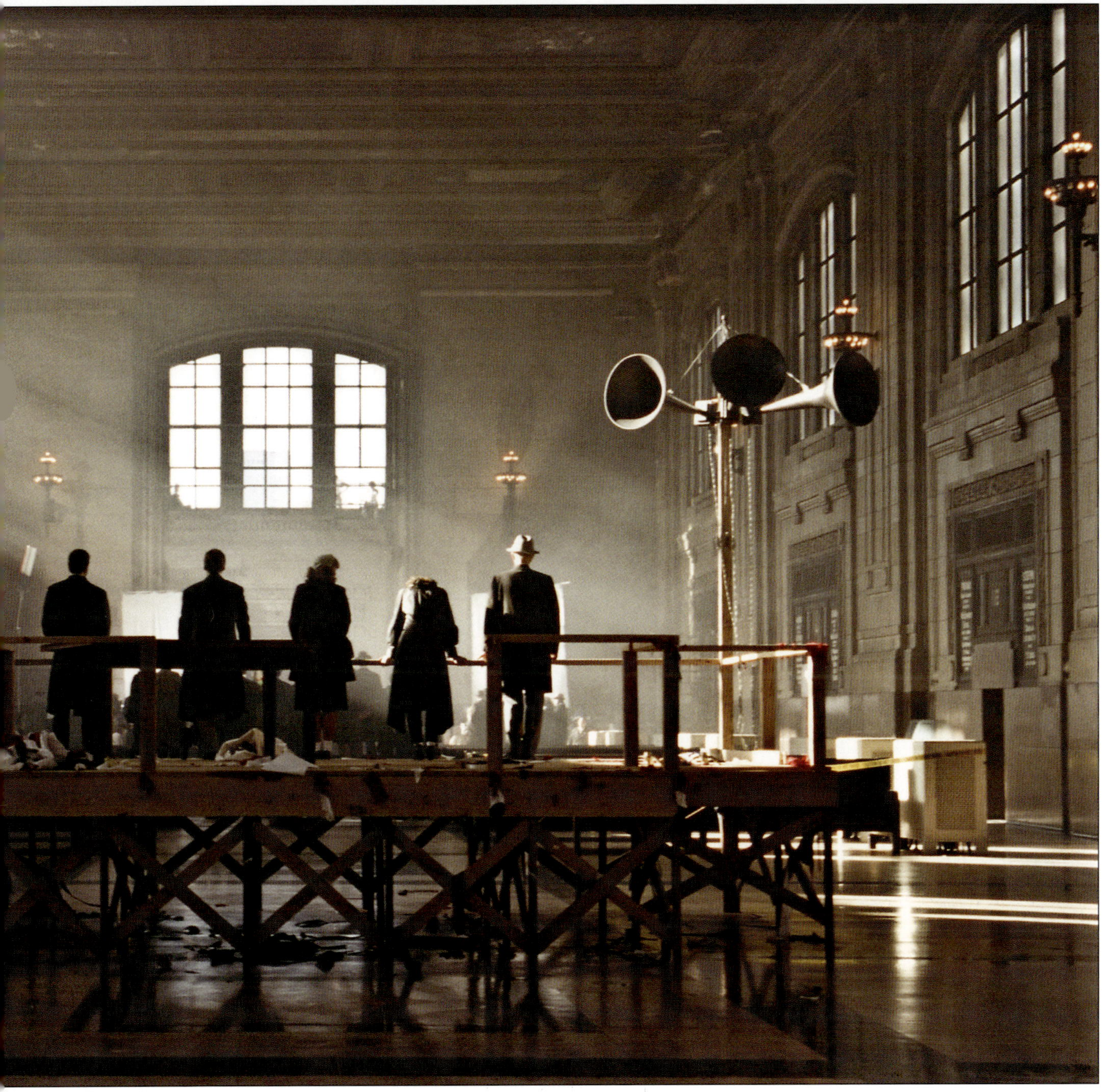

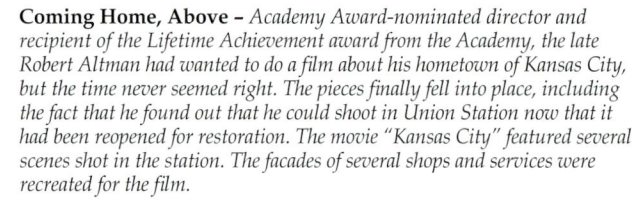

Coming Home, Above – Academy Award-nominated director and recipient of the Lifetime Achievement award from the Academy, the late Robert Altman had wanted to do a film about his hometown of Kansas City, but the time never seemed right. The pieces finally fell into place, including the fact that he found out that he could shoot in Union Station now that it had been reopened for restoration. The movie "Kansas City" featured several scenes shot in the station. The facades of several shops and services were recreated for the film.

Marshalling Forces, Right – As movies were being made inside, construction crews began arriving outside for the imminent restoration process.

One Word: "Plastic," Far Right – By the mid 1970s, plastic chairs had replaced the vintage wooden benches. The chairs had at least two advantages over the benches: they required little maintenance and were not as comfortable for the homeless to nap on. Photo by Charlie Brenneke.

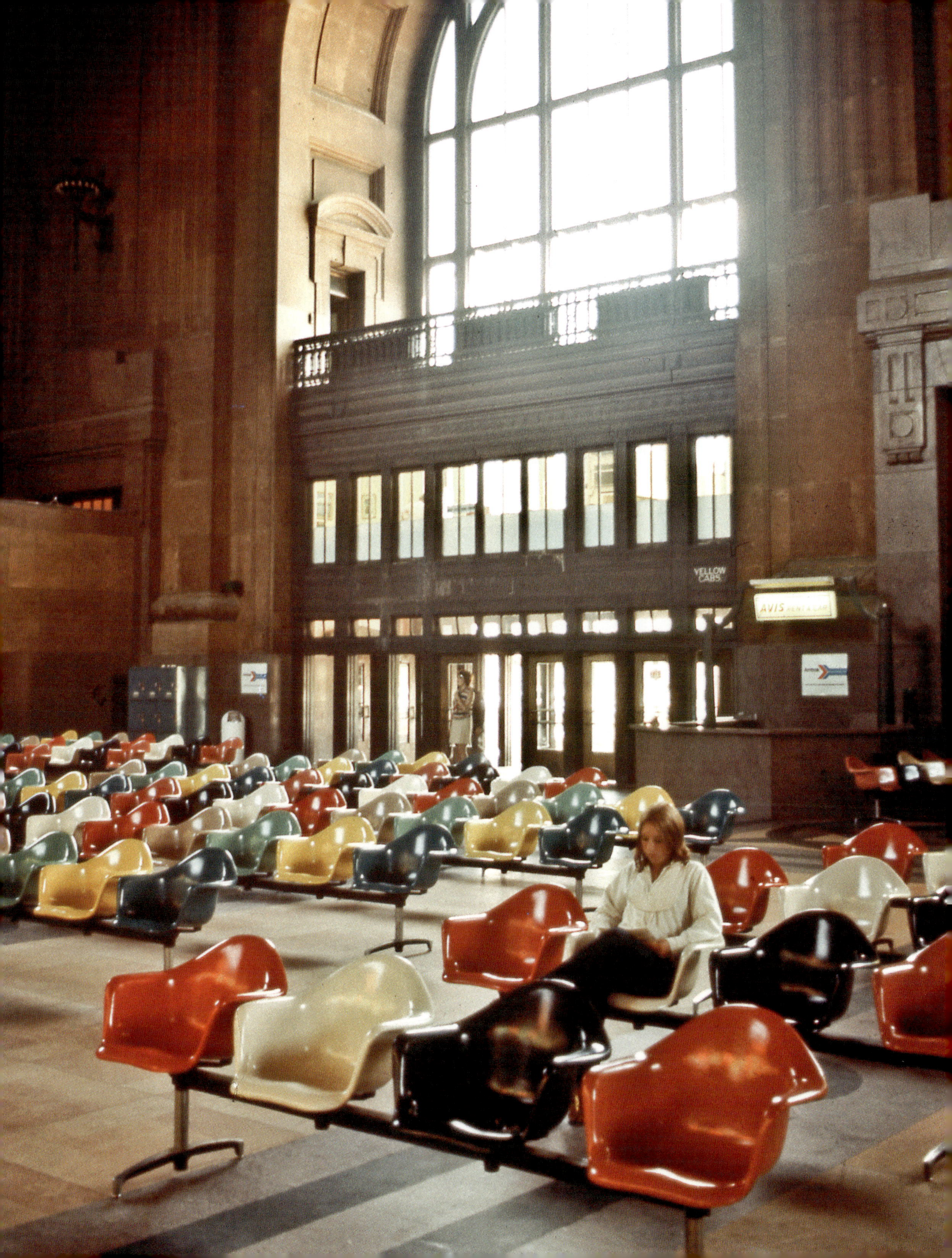
YELLOW CABS.
AVIS

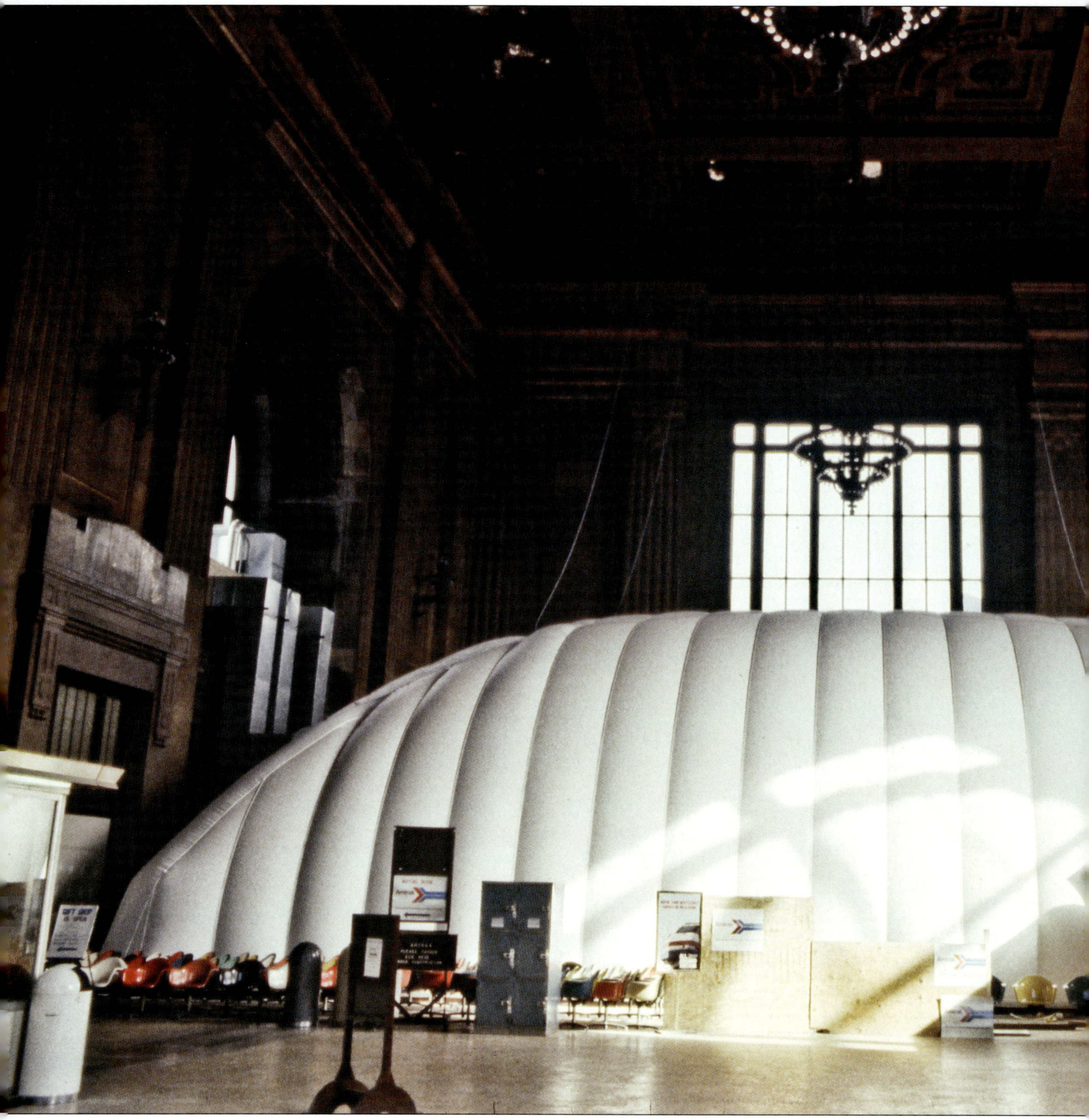

Continued from page 28

and development of a science center. While naysayers were wary of the idea, it had support from high places. Even newsman Walter Cronkite, a former Kansas City resident, came to town to urge approval of the tax to save Union Station.

On Nov. 5, 1996, the community's affection for Union Station was perhaps never more pronounced. Voters backed the tax by 60 percent or better majorities in Jackson, Johnson, Clay and Platte counties, with only Wyandotte County turning it down.

At long last, there was money to bring the beloved Union Station back to life. But keeping the new station viable would be another task altogether.

The White Corpse, Left – *The infamous Amtrak bubble was inflated in the Grand Hall in 1983 in order to keep waiting passengers comfortable. Heating had been turned off in the station. The inflatable was short-lived, because just a year after local rail fan Tom Taylor shot this photo in 1984, Amtrak had left the station and took up residence in the so-called "Amshak" on Main Street several hundred feet east of the station.*

Amshaked, Below – *Dubbed the "Amshak" among other insults, the kit building at the south end of the Main Street overpass was the passenger terminal from 1985 until Amtrak moved back into Union Station in 2002. The entrance from the train was situated under the Main overpass at track level and did not present a particularly attractive welcome to Kansas City.*

34

Chapter 3
The Demolition and The Restoration

At last, Union Station had a future. Voter approval of a bi-state sales tax in 1996 to pay for renovation of the station promised new life for the deserted and decaying landmark. The plans included a museum in the station called Science City, three theaters and as many as 20 new restaurants and shops around the Grand Hall. Construction of the science museum annex and renovation of the station began in January 1998, with a goal of reopening the station in November 1999. But the task proved as large as Union Station itself.

More than 80 years had taken a toll on Union Station, much of it out of view. The walls, floors and ceilings hid decades of wear from a leaky roof and harsh conditions in a building unheated for 15 years. Beams were rusted and girders broken loose. In some places, concrete around the support system came apart in large flakes. Cracked floors had to be replaced, plaster walls recast and a new heating and cooling system installed in the cavernous structure. Outside the building, workers boring holes for the foundation of Science City struck rock-like obstacles and had to use more costly drilling equipment. Several unexpected problems surfaced daily, requiring weekly meetings of design and construction crews to review the repair lists. New construction in such an old building was like trying to put a new shopping center inside a Greek urn, the project manager said at the time.

None of the work that went into the station got as much attention as the remaking of the 95-foot-high ceiling in the Grand Hall. The ceiling had been the station's most decorative feature, with colorful, plastered swirls depicting ribbons, eggs, oak leaves and rosette medallions. But years of neglect in the empty building caused about one-fourth of the ceiling décor to crash to the floor. Only four businesses in the world were qualified to repair the ceiling, project managers said, and only two bid on the $1.5 million job. Working painstakingly atop a maze of scaffolding nearly 100 feet high, artisans recreated the missing ceiling sections to look as exactly like the original design. Many other features of the station, including the

Continued on page 36

The Day Before – *Lloyd Dillinger agreed to recreate for a photo his role as maintenance supervisor, chief cook and bottle washer at Union Station during the dark years when it was abandoned. His tenure at the station went back much further than that. Lloyd had started with the Kansas City Terminal Railway in 1964. Both before and after, he did much more than push around an ancient cart; he knew the station like the back of his hand. This likeness was struck in 1996, after the passage of the historic bi-state cultural tax and the very day before construction crews and craftsmen moved inside to begin the demolition and restoration. Note the deteriorated ceiling and the train announcement boards that were leftovers from the two movie shoots of 1995.*

Continued from page 35

ornate copper light fixtures and brass door hardware, were refurbished. Even the famed clock, 6 ½ feet in diameter, was taken down and shipped out for expert restoration.

At a cost of $250 million, Union Station would become the highest-priced renovation of an historic building in Kansas City history and the region's second-largest private fundraising effort. Private foundations, companies and individuals donated about $100 million for the restoration. It also received $32 million in federal funds. The station was much changed from its heyday before World War II, when hundreds of trains passed through each day. There were no more stairs to the trains, no platforms or tracks. Parts of those spaces were used for Science City and other new construction.

As the grand reopening of Union Station approached in the fall of 1999, some work was still not complete, including office and

Continued on page 46

An Ugly Start, Clockwise from upper left – Before the beginning of the restoration there was the demolition. This is what the Grand Hall looked like as crews worked to remove pieces of the decayed plaster ceiling, a 60 percent restoration project. This process created a lot of dust that in turn required a continuous string of cleanup people, some of whom were assembling to start their day's work.

It was a LONG way down from the dizzying height nearly 90 feet off the floor.

On top of the temporary and rickety scaffolding, the raw, exposed steel supports for the ceiling can be seen up close as a worker finishes cleaning up one section.

After the demolition phase, the ceiling was an ugly sight from below.

Up To The Task – *A much larger and more substantial scaffolding went up in the Grand Hall to allow artisans and craftsmen to begin their work.*

Above – *Bill Ehlers, a master artisan at his craft, led a crew that painstakingly applied several coats of paint to faithfully recreate the lavish Beau Arts ceiling centerpiece.*

At right – *Those are the hands of a master at the craft of plastering, Julian Davis. He worked for Hayles & Howe, the England-based company tasked with rebuilding the iconic ceilings of Union Station. He was nicknamed "Chewy" as a youth because he had long hair extending down his back, resembling the Star Wars character. Julian possessed the unique skill to recreate the eggs and beam casings from what remained of the originals. This was no simple feat, as the originals were not of uniform size. In the adjoining photo, workers carefully raised a plaster piece for installation.*

Center right – *The ceiling is finished and awaits the arrival and installation of the chandeliers.*

Far right – *With the successful installation of a large piece, two plasterers congratulated each other.*

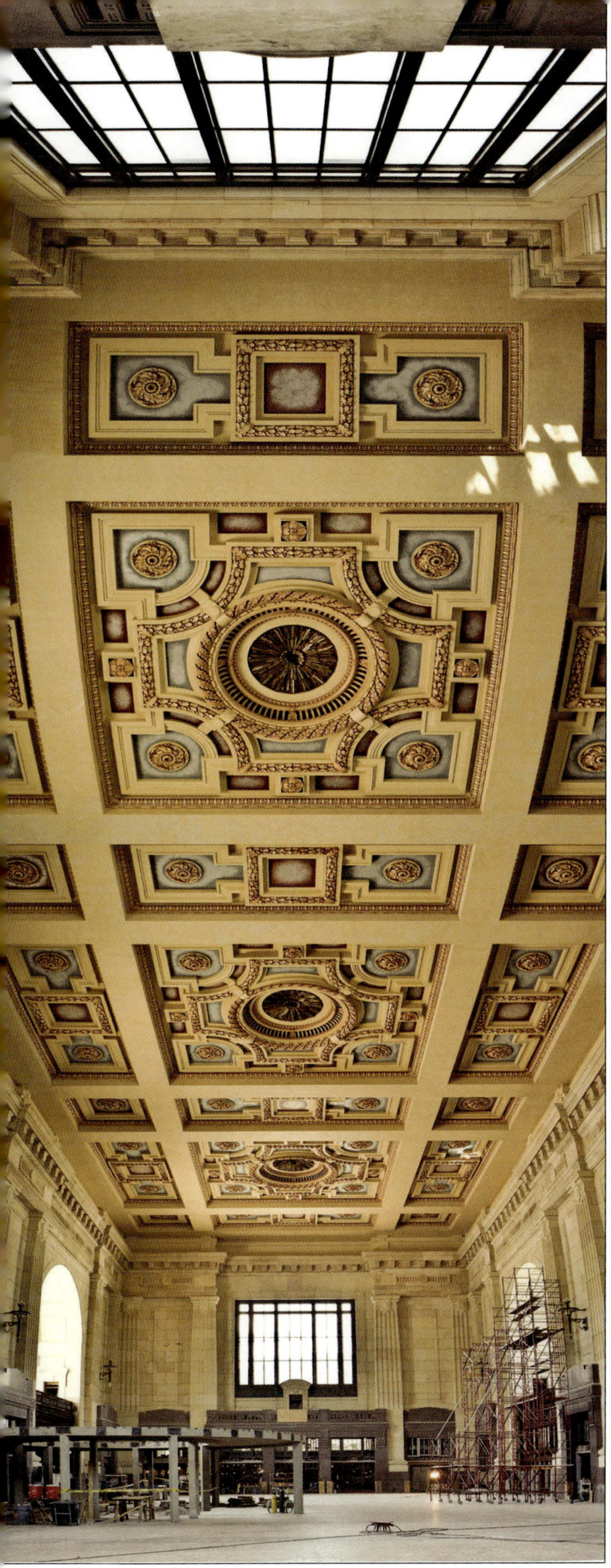

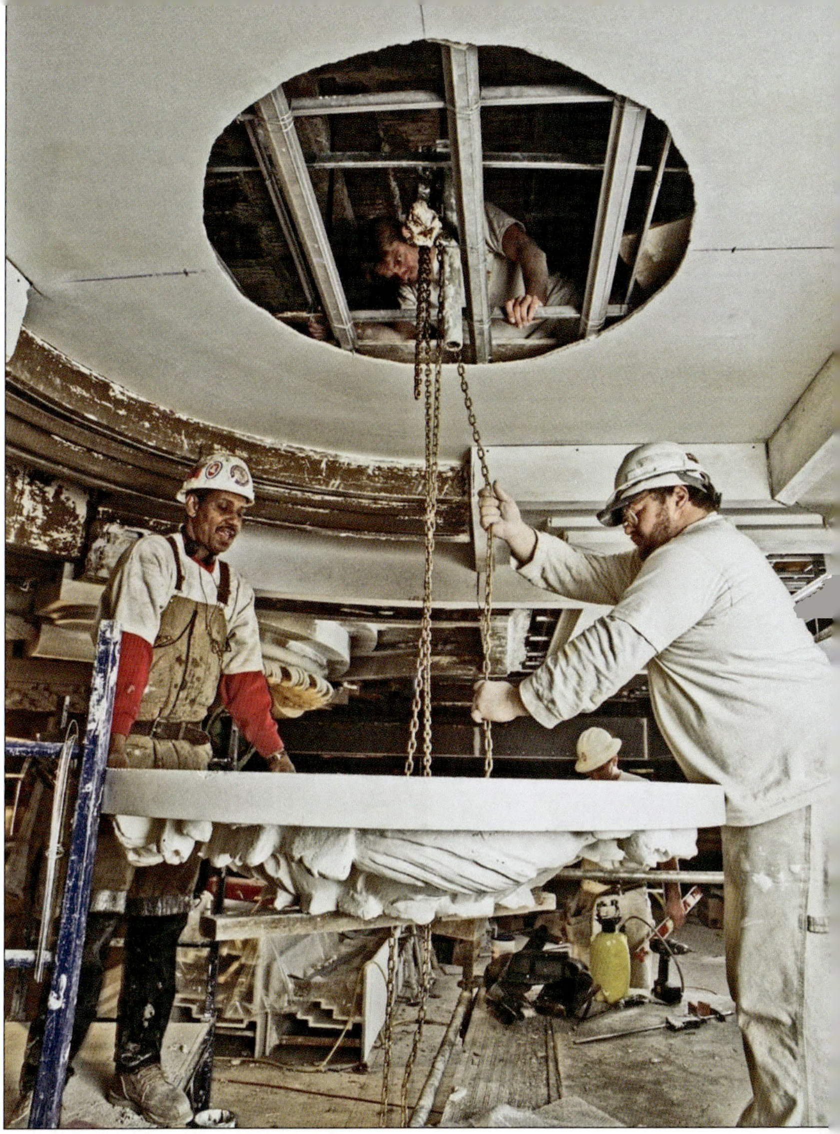

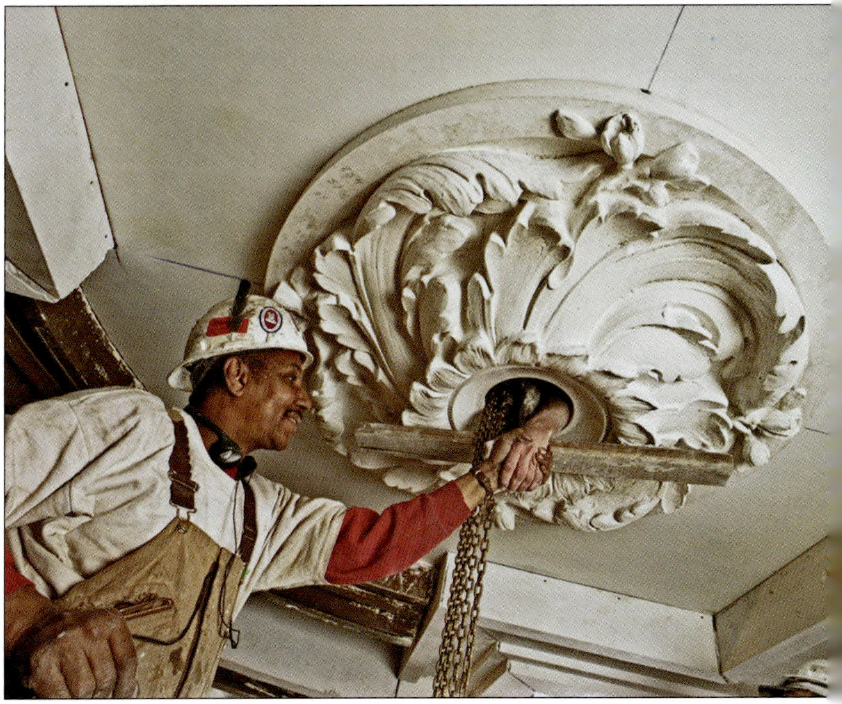

Leaving Their Marks, Above – *Modern craftsmen used a black marker pen to record their names on the final rosette to be installed in the Grand Hall ceiling. Photographer Roy Inman and his first assistant George Inman were also invited to include their names on that last piece of the ceiling puzzle.*

Right – *As was the custom in a previous century, workers and craftsmen sometimes left their names scratched on a piece of plaster for posterity at the conclusion of a major project. In a wonderfully fortuitous stroke of luck, demolition workers discovered that Union Station architect Jarvis Hunt inscribed his name as well. This piece of damaged plaster was saved during the demolition phase and is in the station archives.*

THE DEMOLITION AND THE RESTORATION   41

The Missing Stripe, Left – *In the North Waiting Room (Sprint Festival Plaza, as it's now known), there was a stripe that was supposed to have been painted on the ceiling but wasn't. Bill Ehlers, shown in the foreground, and his associates had finished the masterful colorizing of the 350-foot-by-85-foot waiting room ceiling – or so they thought. Bill related: "I was literally walking out with an empty paint can and my clean brushes when architectural preservation consultant Mary Oehrlein came running up to me and pointing to the ceiling, excitedly asked, 'Where is the neutral brown stripe on the outside of the rectangle!?' I asked her WHAT stripe? And she proceeded to show me the revised specs, which somehow had not gotten to me, and sure enough, there it was." Oehrlein and her associates had arduously scraped a total of more than 200 paint chip samples from both the North Waiting Room and Grand Hall ceilings to determine as closely as humanly possible the correct, original colors. There was no written record of those colors, and of course there was no color photography in 1914 to document them.*

Below – *The massive scaffolding, shown here in an early, partially-constructed state, had been removed from the North Waiting Room and was now being erected in the Grand Hall in preparation for the restoration of that ceiling. A rickety, much smaller, rolling scaffolding was assembled. It had an outside rung ladder, no safety net, going straight up. Once on top, the plywood platform was not very large and jiggled. In order to get a sharp photo, the painters as well as the photographer had to pause and hold their collective breaths during the exposure.*

Big Lights, Clockwise From Top – *Each 3,000-pound chandelier, attached to steel beams in the attic, was lowered close to the floor and inspected. Project manager Donald McCormick stood on a sawhorse for a closer look.*

One of three hand cranks that required two men to operate remains intact in the attic. Union Station A/V & Exhibit Specialist Nickolas Cline demonstrated how it was used to lower and raise each chandelier.

During the restoration, an electric winch was installed to get the big fixtures down to change the burned-out bulbs. Station engineers were nervous, however: If they got the chandeliers down, would the winches be strong enough to get them back up? Or would they come crashing to the floor? Some brave soul gave it a go: down and up, no harm. BUT it took nearly all day to winch down a single chandelier and about the same amount of time to bring it back up.

It took a crew of Capital Electric workers to wrestle each chandelier into the proper position for installation.

Today the preferred method to change out the energy efficient CFL (compact fluorescent lamps) is with a bucket lift, operated here with a deft touch by the station's Ruben Diaz.

The Demolition and the Restoration 43

Photo Fusion – *On occasion, the artifacts of restoration merged with the Beau Arts architecture, creating a third effect that presented its own unique visual statement. This image was captured from the west roof of the Midway just before sunset, when the light was balanced enough to create a warm reflection in the northwest arched window and allowed the interior scaffolding under construction inside to be seen.*

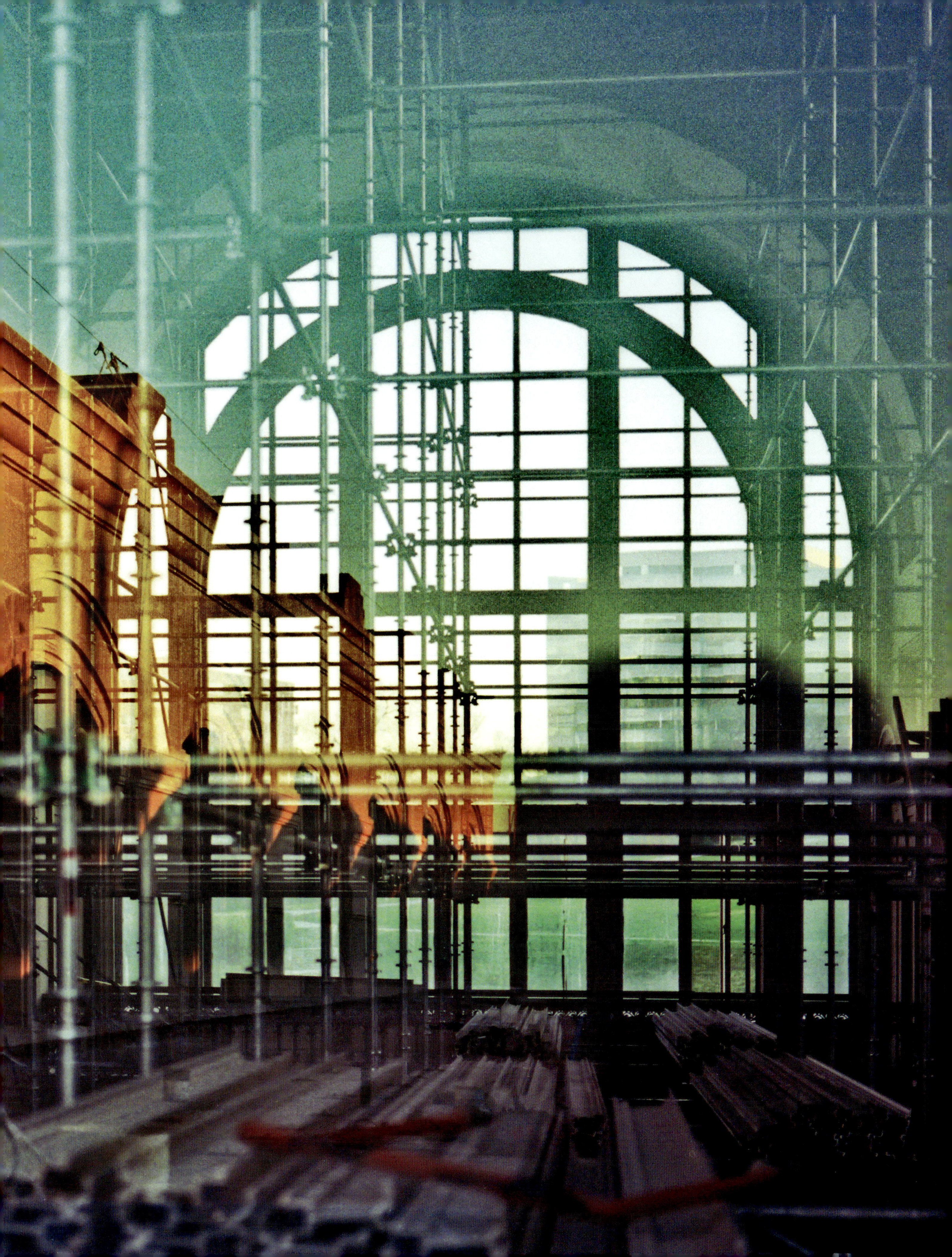

Continued from page 36

retail space and a glass overhead walkway linking the station to the hotel and shops of Crown Center. But those delays did nothing to temper the station's glitzy debut on Nov. 4, 1999. A dinner and cocktail party honored those who donated at least $100,000 to the restoration. One attendee, Drue Jennings, co-chairman of the capital campaign, called the dazzling transformation of the long-closed station "remarkable, awesome and intimidating." An invited guest that night was retired CBS News anchor Walter Cronkite, who was a reporter in Kansas City in the 1930s and a strong advocate of renovating the station. It happened to be his 83rd birthday, and 600 or so people regaled Cronkite with a "Happy Birthday" song around dinner tables in the giant North Waiting Room. Several more days of gala events followed. The revered station was once again a social

Continued on page 58

Stairway to Splendor – *The Grand Stairs were added during the restoration and now connect the theater level with the Grand Hall. Anthony Benton Gude, grandson of famed regionalist painter Thomas Hart Benton, created the colorful, 8.5-foot-by-30-foot mural above the stairs in the same fluid style made popular by his grandfather. The mural depicts locomotives from the 12 railroads that financed construction of Union Station. Kansas City Southern's board of directors funded the work in 2006 and was donated to Union Station in the name of Mike Haverty, the railroad's chairman, president and CEO.*

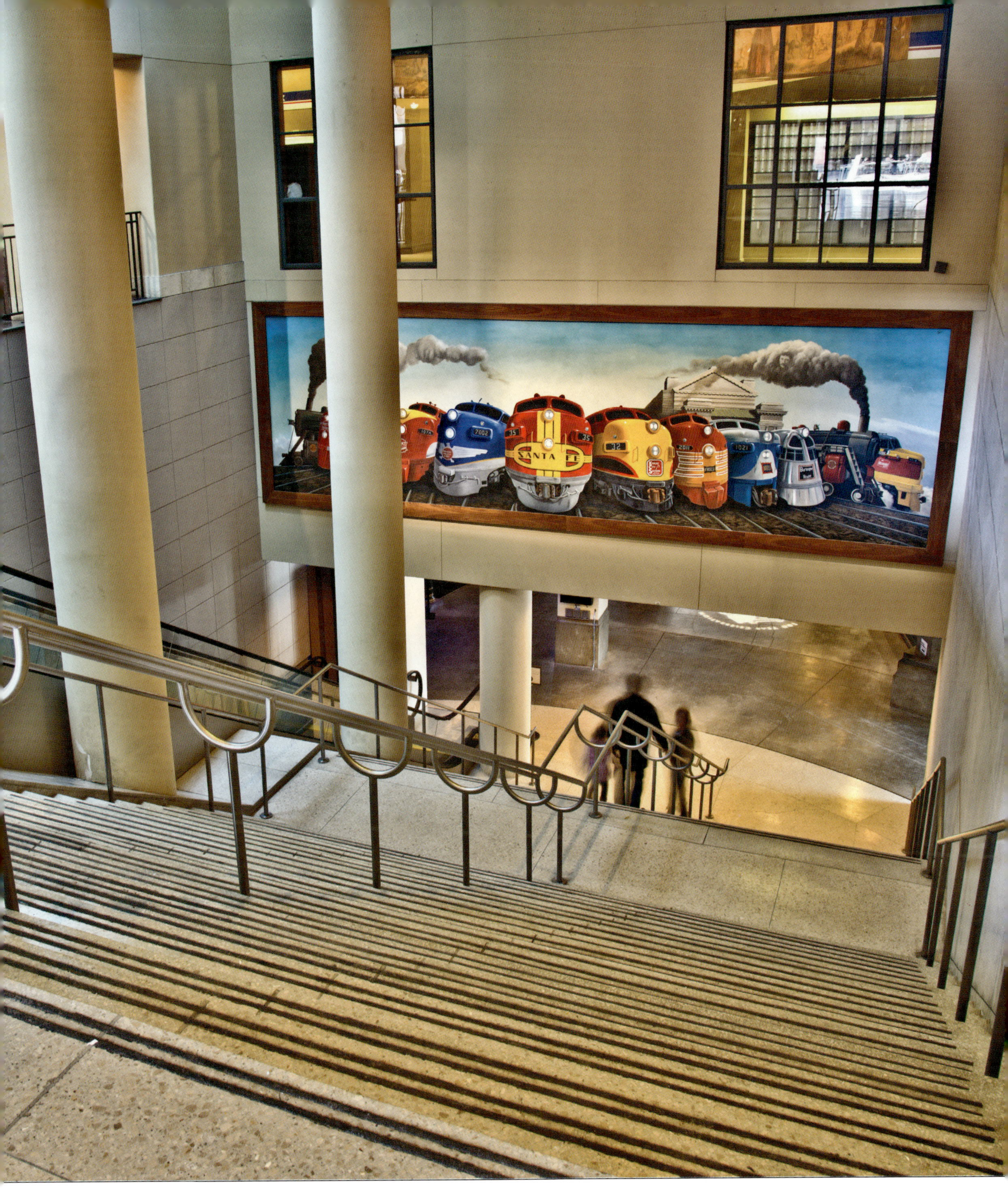
SANTA FE

The Dirty Nitty-Gritty – *Somewhere between B and A levels on the east side, an entire floor had to be demolished.*

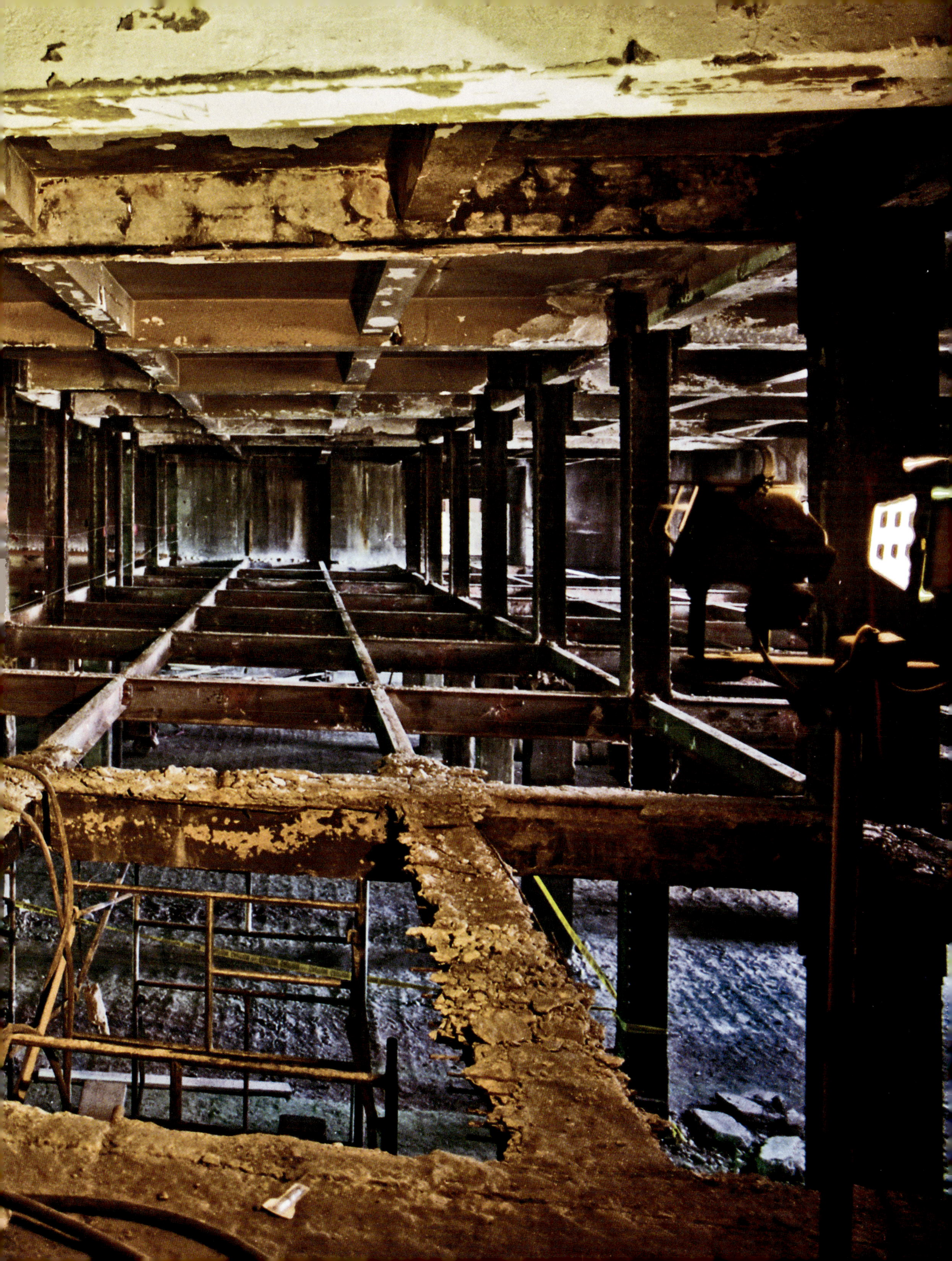

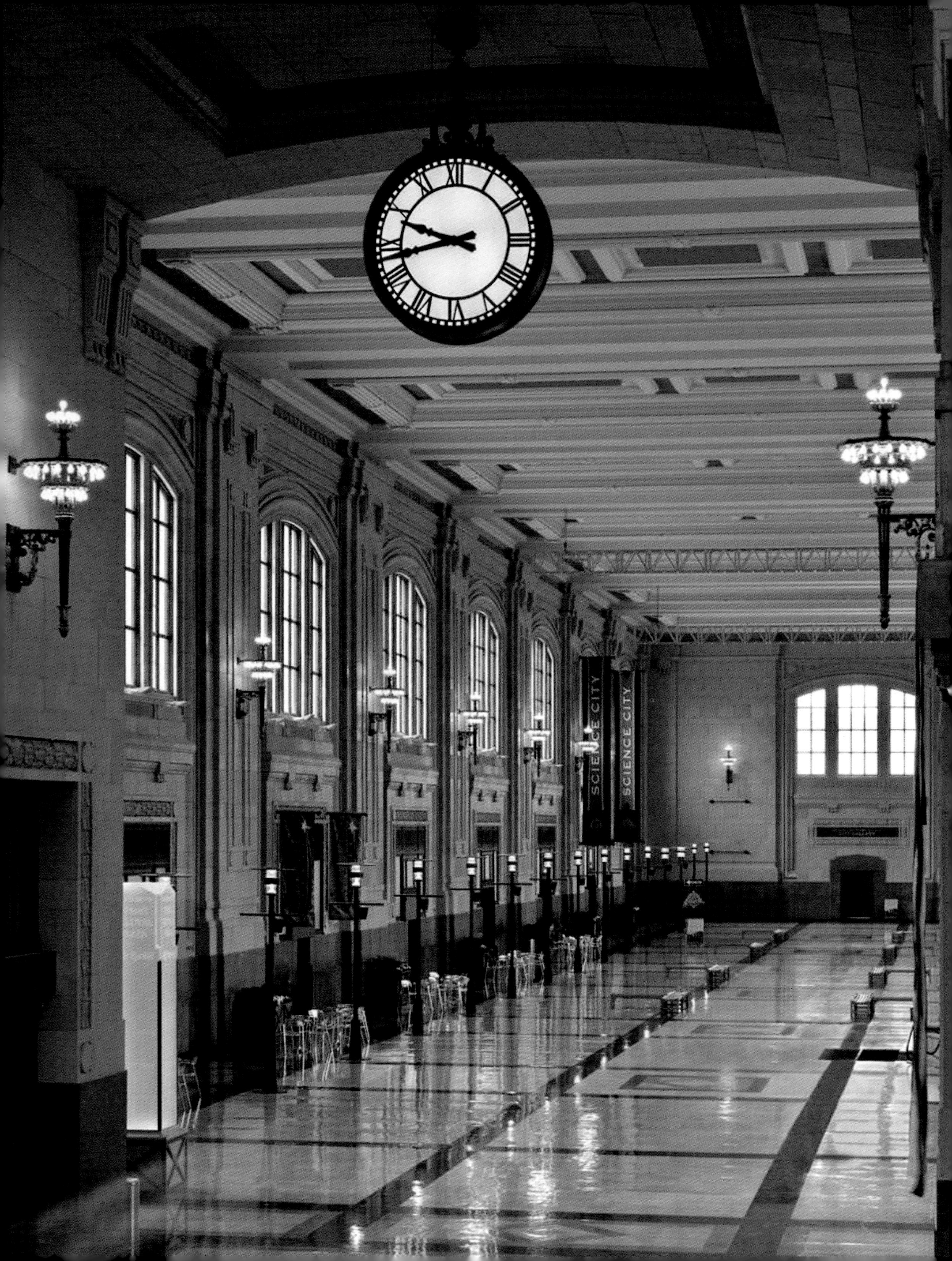
SCIENCE CITY
SCIENCE CITY

THE DEMOLITION AND THE RESTORATION   51

How It Works, Left – There is no timekeeping mechanism as such inside the clock. That task is handled by a computer-controlled devise in the attic space above the arch. Union Station AV Tech and Building Engineer Troyce Holliman looks it over. There are "motion works" inside the big clock that keep all four hands synchronized on both clock faces. The devise above the arch is connected to the clock below by a drive shaft running through the floor/ceiling. The clock is automatically adjusted for Daylight Savings Time, and in case of a power outage, resets when power is restored. During the restoration, Dave Falke of The Clock Shop in Kansas City, **photo above,** donated his time to help bring the iconic timepiece back to life.

Time-Keeper for a Century, Far Left – The single best-known and also the most revered feature of Union Station is the famous, double-faced clock that hangs from the arch leading into Festival Plaza. "Meet me under the clock" was and has again become a catch phrase in the lexicon of Kansas Citians.

Top Left – The big timepiece came with no directions for removal. A number of options were discussed, including hacking into the arch ceiling. No one liked that idea. A Capital Electric electrician discovered that there was a large retaining ring at the clock's mounting point. He spun it, it unscrewed, and voila! The 6.5-foot, 1,000-pound timepiece dropped – but only a few feet. Most fortunately, a scaffolding with a cushion had been built around the clock, so no harm was done. But there were a few anxious seconds for those watching. The iconic symbol of Union Station was removed in March 1998, shipped to a clock repair company in Massachusetts and returned to the station.

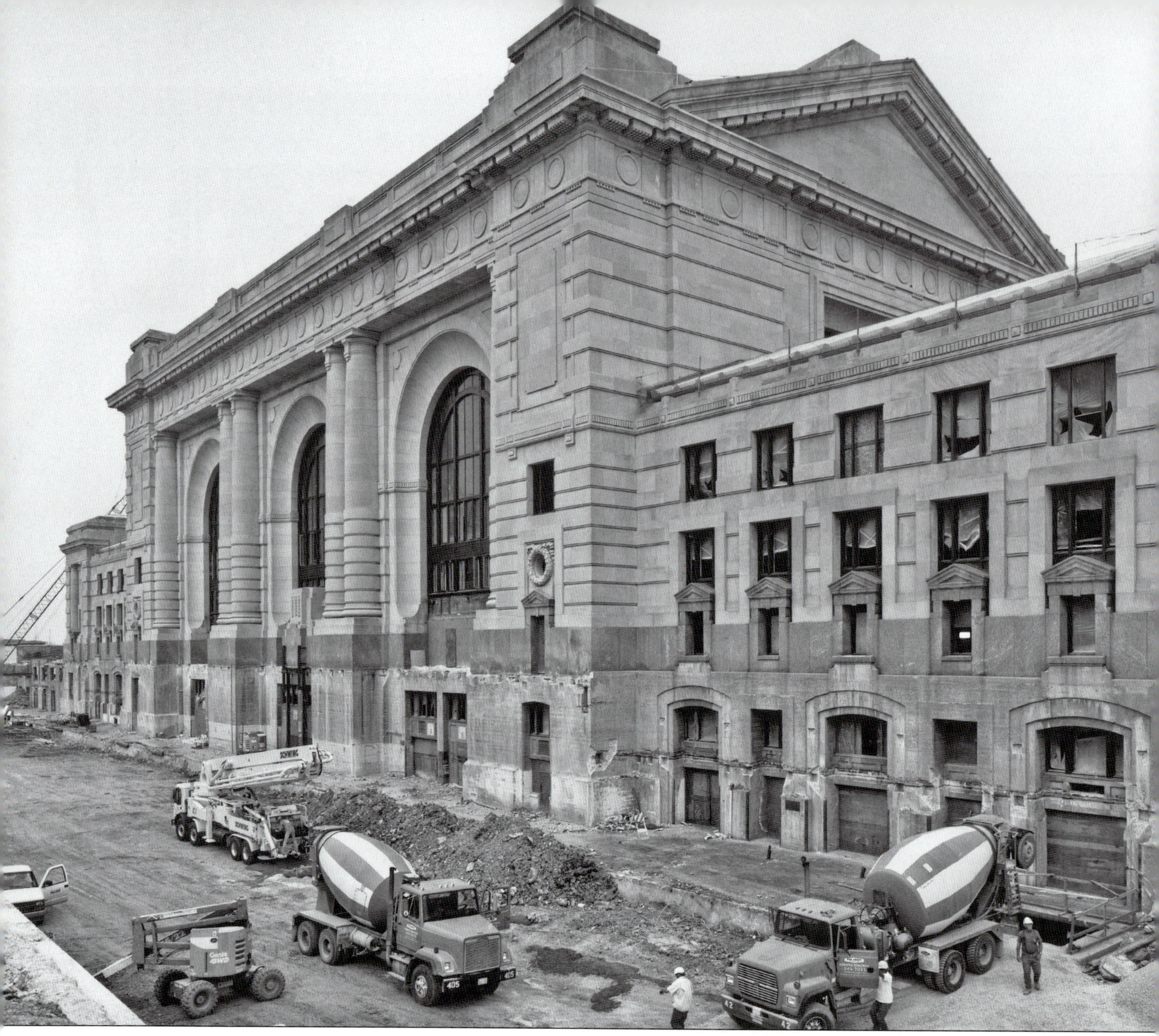

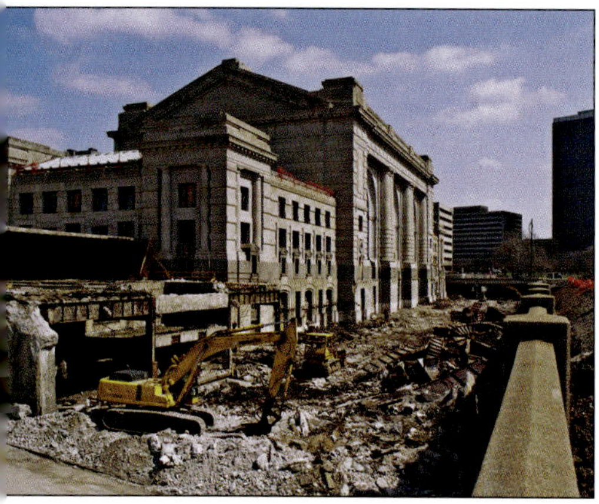

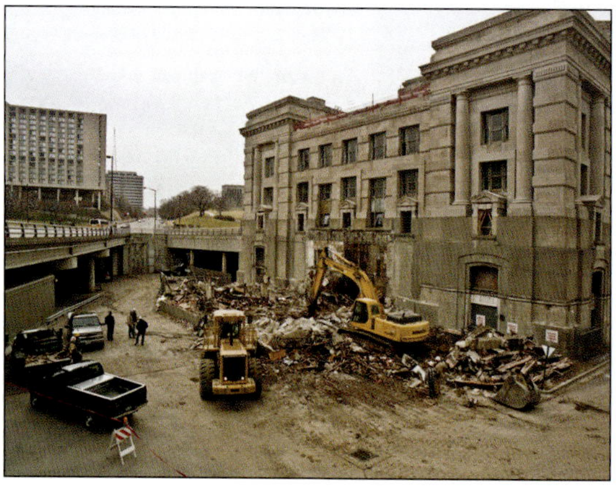

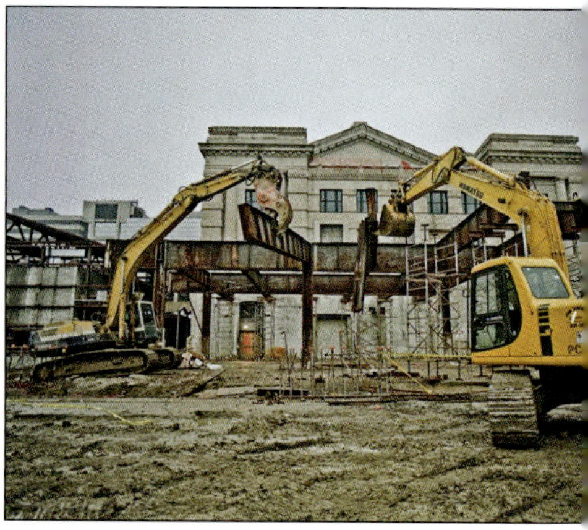

THE DEMOLITION AND THE RESTORATION   53

Debris and Cool Doors, Clockwise From Top Left – *Compared to the massive Union Station, full-sized cement trucks looked like toys as they poured material to restore OK Street. The photo is deceptive: The trucks are not on the parking lot level, but one story below.*

Crews placed a concrete support for the west end of the front parking lot.

Both the west and east canopies over the front doors were completely torn up and rebuilt. This photo was taken on what was left of the east canopy.

Brass doors welcome visitors and travelers as they have for 100 years. The decision was made to have the doors refurbished, not replaced, maintaining their well-used look and feel.

The front parking lot had been partially removed in this photo.

The final three photos document the demolition of the Carriage Pavilion, the Fred Harvey commissary and the west end of the parking lot.

Before, During, and After, Above and Right – *What was once the Women's Waiting Room is now Pierpont's restaurant in the northeast corner of the Grand Hall. Before and after photos illustrate the stunning transformation.*

Top Right – *At the opposite end of the Grand Hall from Pierpont's are now a set of men's and women's restrooms, shown here in the ugly demolition phase.*

Far Right – *Additional lighting was added to the North Waiting Room to more properly create the illusion of an outdoor space in Sprint Festival Plaza.*

Center Right – *The inside walls and ceiling of the station were thoroughly cleaned using a biodegradable, non-toxic solution. The difference between the cleaned and non-cleaned areas is striking.*

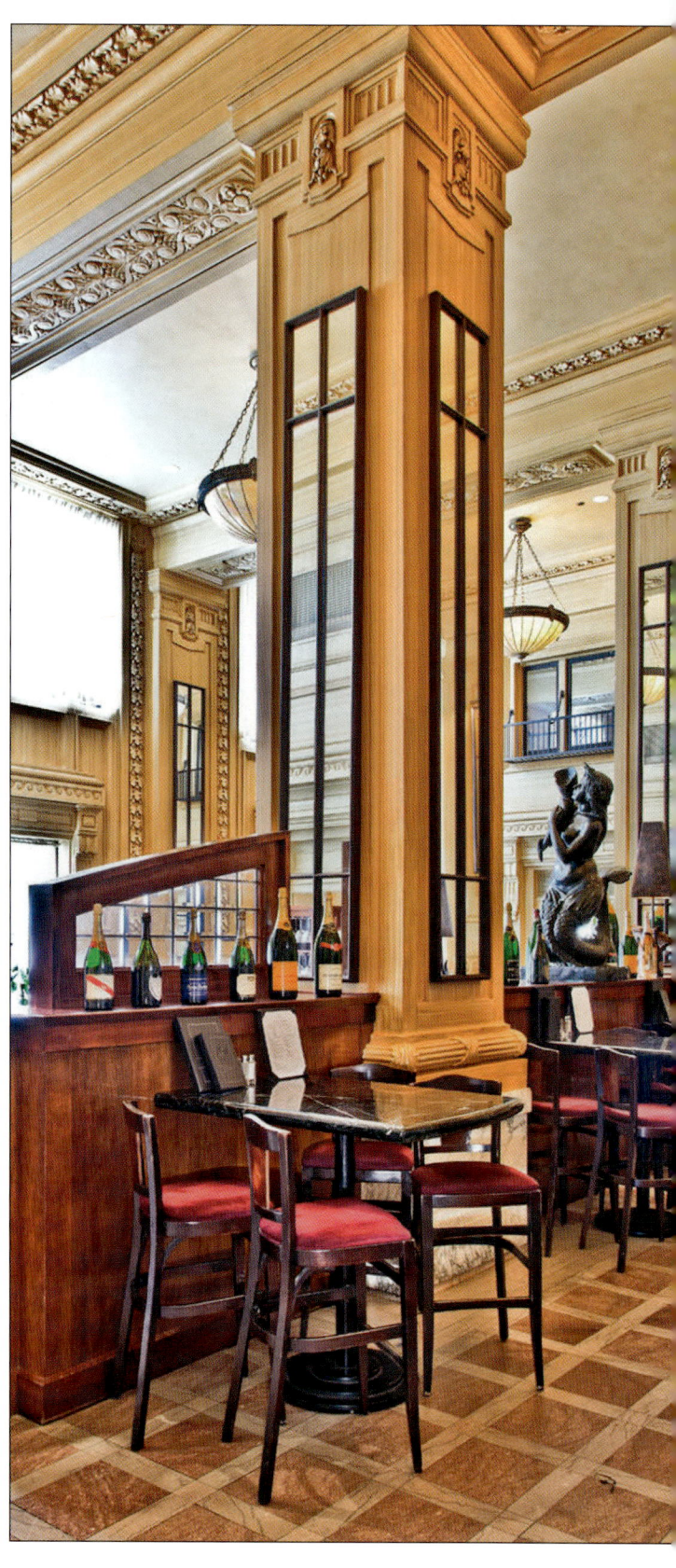

The Demolition and the Restoration 55

Above It All, Top – New tiles and roofing materials were hoisted to the roof.

Above – Workers on the Grand Hall roof had a panoramic view of the city as they completed their task.

Right – At 200 pounds, the new tiles being set in place weighed half that of the old ones, thanks to the then relatively-new technique of fusing concrete and fiberglass. They were fabricated at a plant in Lincoln, Neb.

Top – *Craftsmen tuckpointed the new tiles. The roof had been a problem since the station was built. After years of neglect, the situation was even worse. The large concrete tiles were cracked, and water seeped in. The waterproof underlayment had long since deteriorated.*

Above – *New guttering is designed to properly direct rainwater from the roof.*

Left – *This is how the roof pieces are attached.*

Continued from page 46
center of the community.

Science City, the marque attraction of the new Union Station, opened to the public on Nov. 11, 1999. The adventure-based museum was heralded as potentially one of the city's biggest cultural attractions as well as a destination for school field trips. The museum – more like a theme park – took visitors along stone streets, building facades and park-like settings in a hands-on journey of discovery. It was considered the next generation of science museums, where interactive exhibits leaned heavily toward entertainment while still teaching visitors about physics, biology and other sciences. The potential popularity of the science museum was unknown, but planners projected 900,000 paying visitors the first year. That was important because Science City was intended to help offset an estimated $2.7 million negative cash flow for the station overall in the first year. Much glee surrounded the reopening of the historic station, but it faced an uphill path to financial viability.

The Scientific Side – *A separate structure attached to the station's North Waiting Room houses Science City. A truss that would be the main building block for Science City was carefully lifted into place. A favorite activity from the start was the cable bike ride. Science on a Sphere is one of the recent additions. The Arvin Gottlieb Planetarium was mondernised in 2010 and resides alongside Science City.*

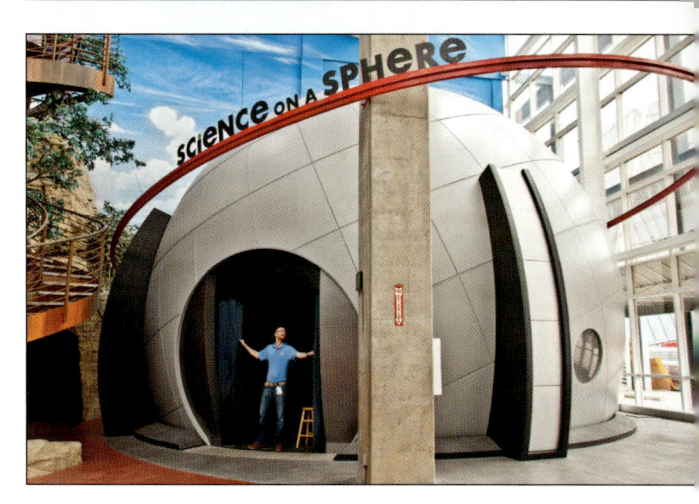

THE DEMOLITION AND THE RESTORATION   59

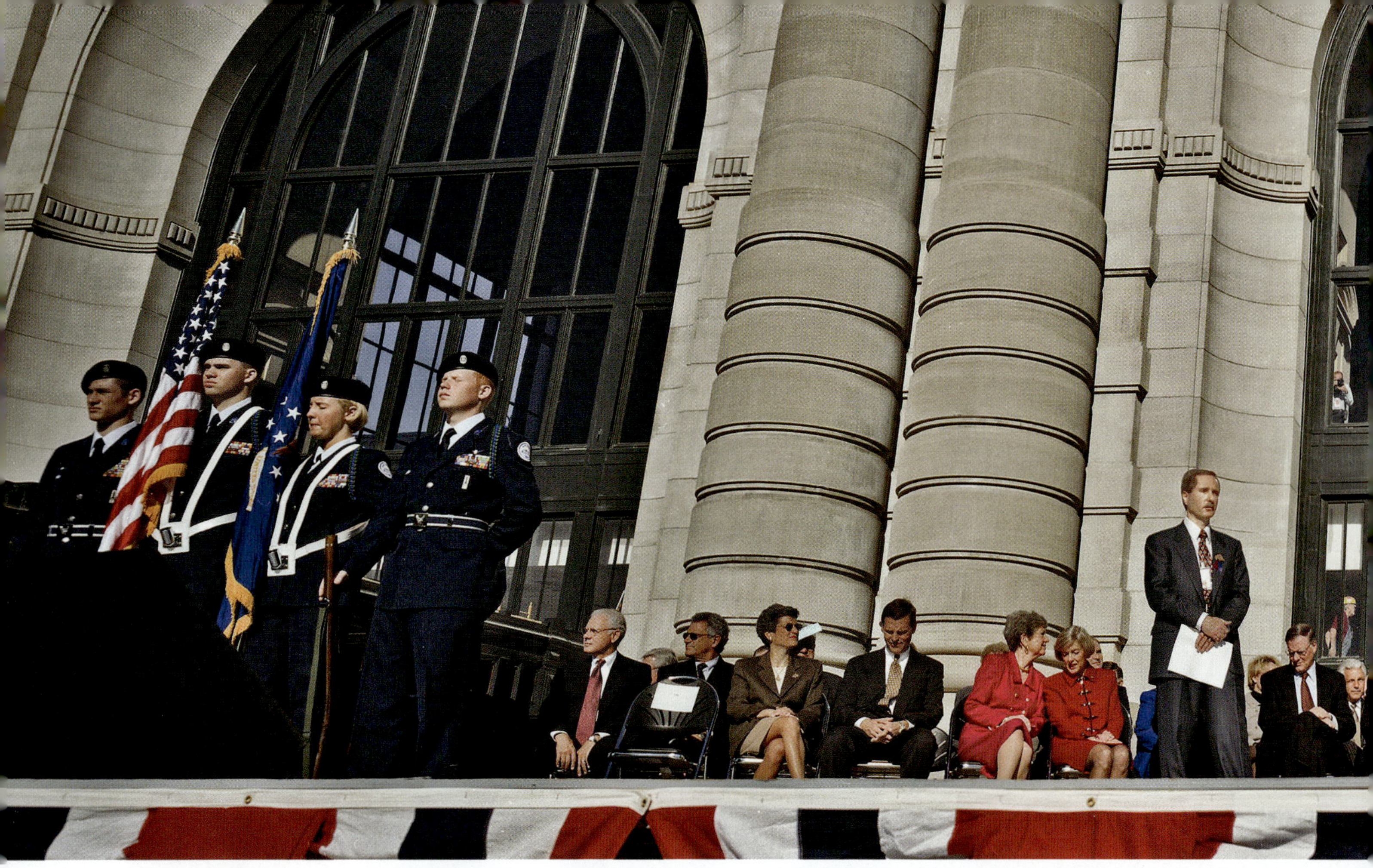
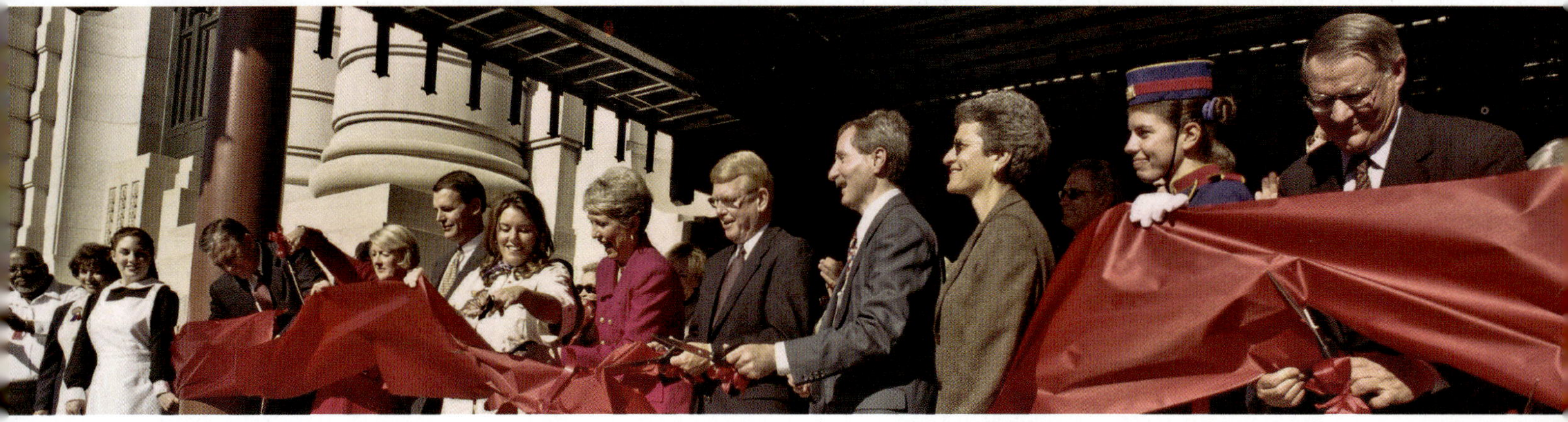
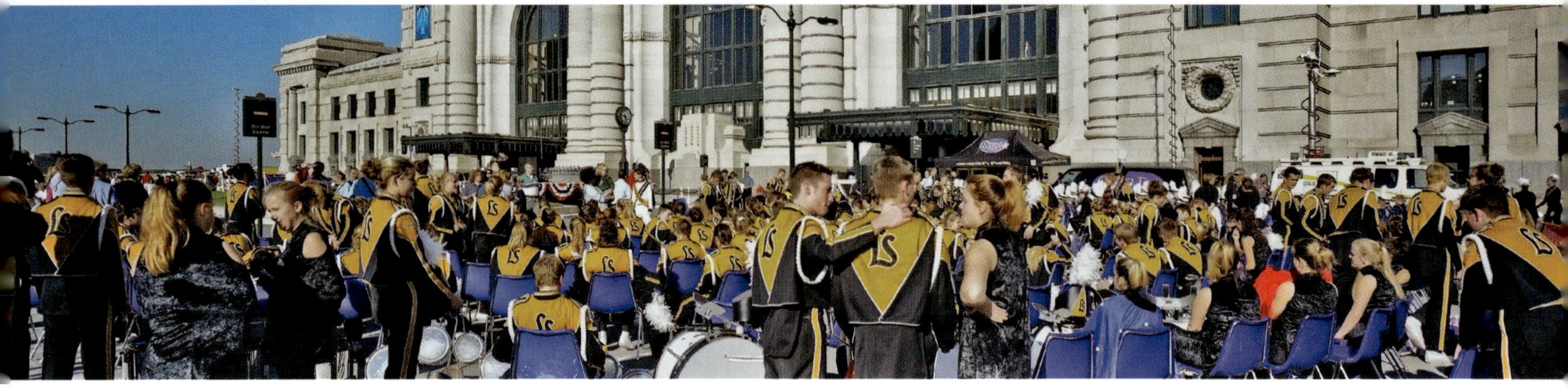

Finally! Clockwise From Top – *Andy Scott, who was executive director of the Union Station Assistance Corporation, is at the podium; David Ucko, Science City president, and other dignitaries spoke.*

It turns out that former Mayor Kay Barnes and her cousin, the late Walter Cronkite, were of the kissing variety, which they demonstrated at the opening gala. It was Cronkite's birthday, and he was treated to cake and ice cream. Cronkite, a Kansas Citian, was a staunch supporter of the restoration of Union Station and had earlier done an ad spot to promote the passage of the historic 1/8th cent bi-state sales tax to help fund the renewal of the station.

Several high schools participated, including the Lee's Summit High School band.

Dignitaries cut ribbons in front of both entrances on opening day, Nov. 10, 1999. This photo shows the moment on the east side.

One Big Party – The grand re-opening had been more than a month earlier, on Nov. 10, 1999, but New Year's Eve attracted a far larger crowd that same year at the station. It was as much a triumphant gathering, expressing sheer joy that the station was finally saved from the wrecking ball, as it was a ringing-in.

The evening was spectacular! There was a party inside. There was a party outside. There were multiple bands that played throughout the night. Thousands turned out. National news media covered the event. Outside there were fireworks to the north and south of the station. Inside, laser lights created a faux fireworks display on the walls of the Grand Hall. And even the weather cooperated for the outdoor revelers: Temperatures were close to 40 degrees, balmy for a Dec. 31st in Kansas City, and winds were calm. When the big clock inside struck midnight, a deafening roar arose from the throng gathered in the Grand Hall, reenacting a nearly century-old beloved tradition.

The year 2000 – bright, shiny and full of promise for the future of the station – had begun with a cascade of thousands of balloons that rained down on an ecstatic crowd. But there would be difficult days ahead for the station: overoptimistic projections for Science City attendance, the 9-11 tragedy that crippled the tourism industry and several station administrations and boards that struggled to make the iconic building financially viable.

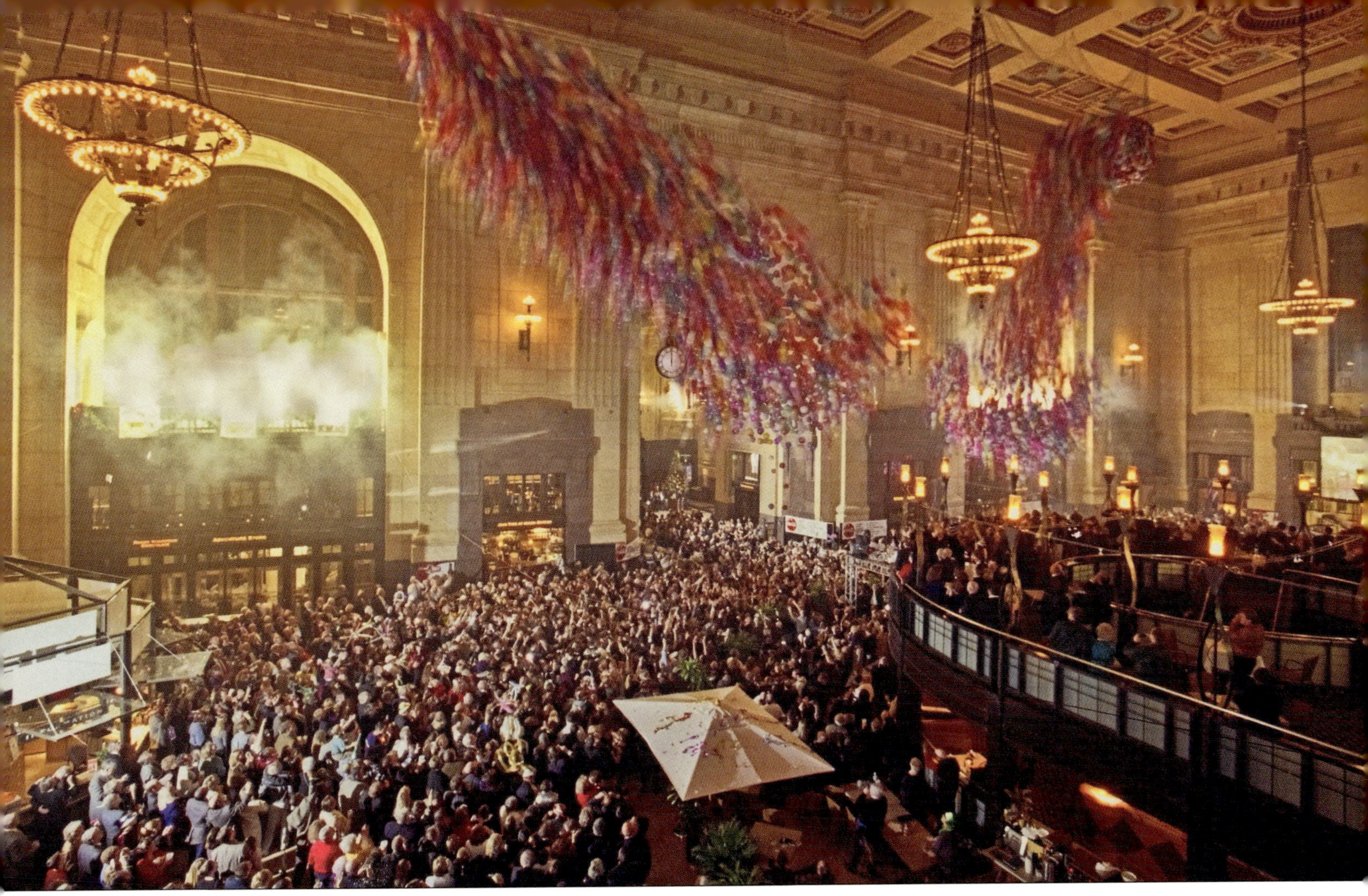

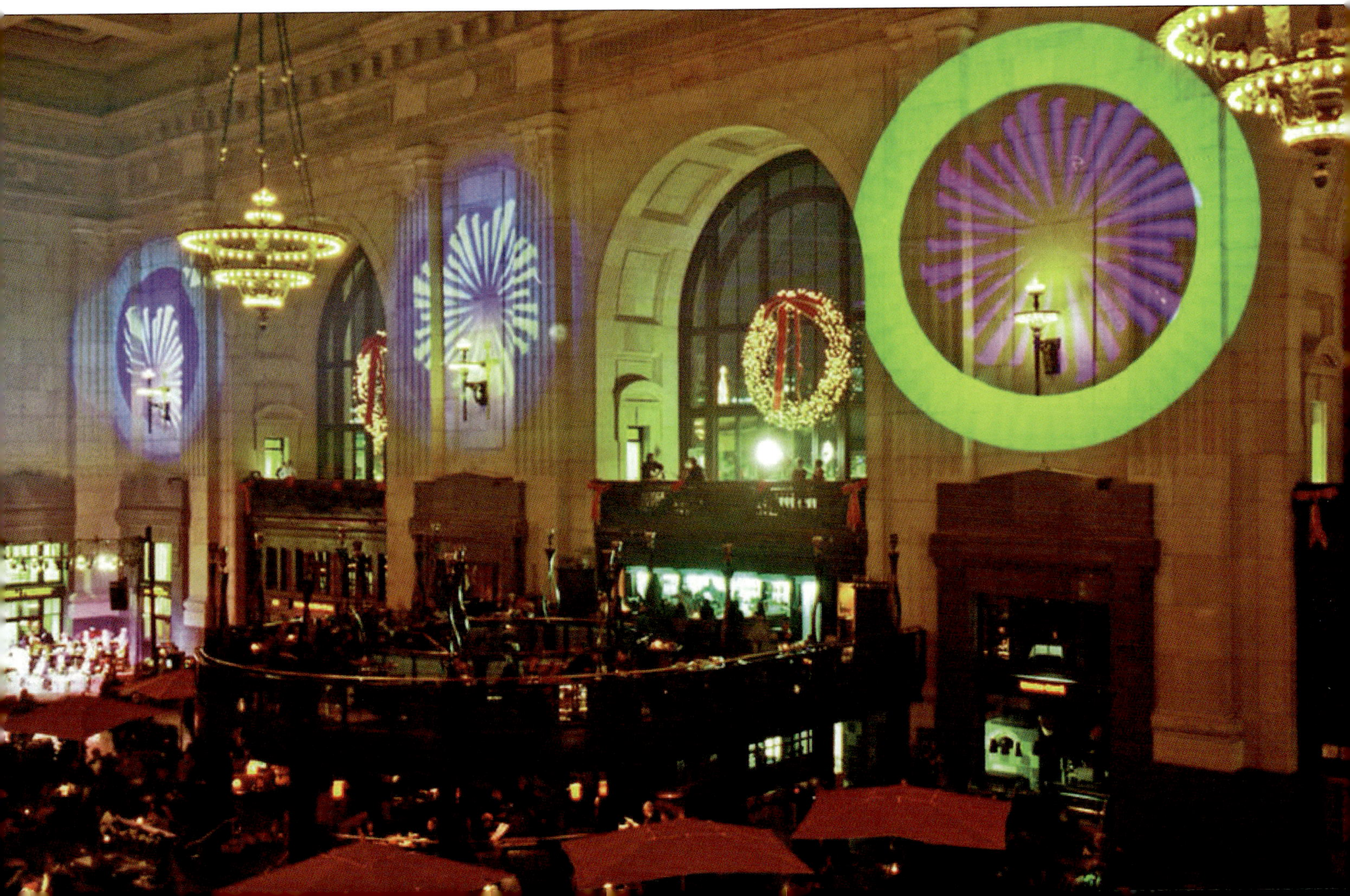

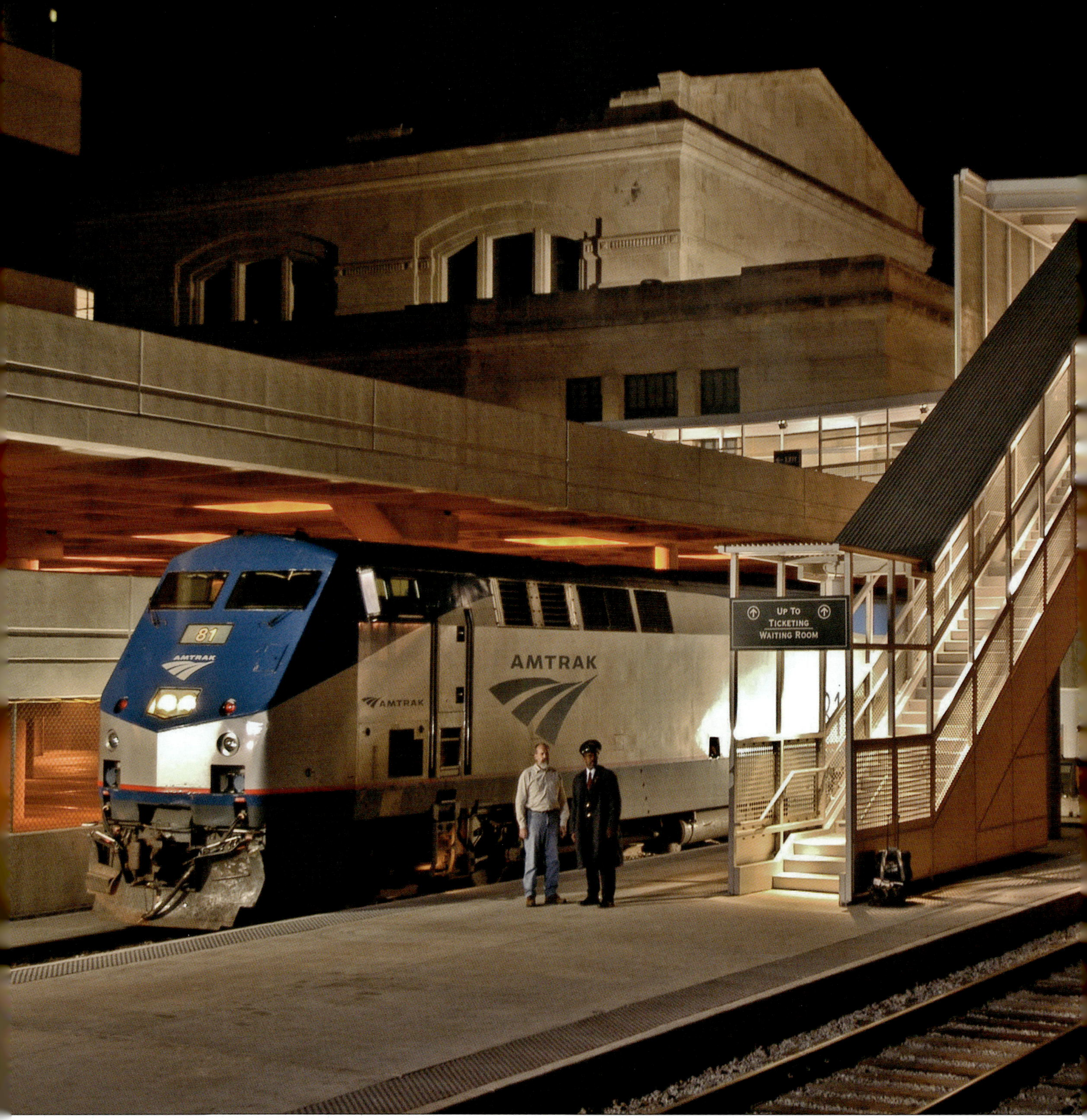
81
AMTRAK
AMTRAK
UP TO
TICKETING
WAITING ROOM

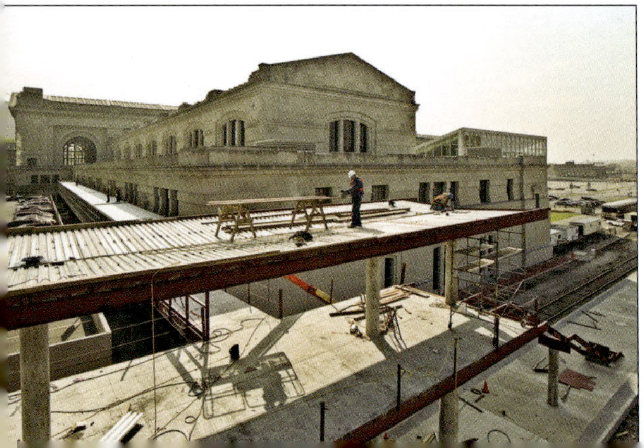

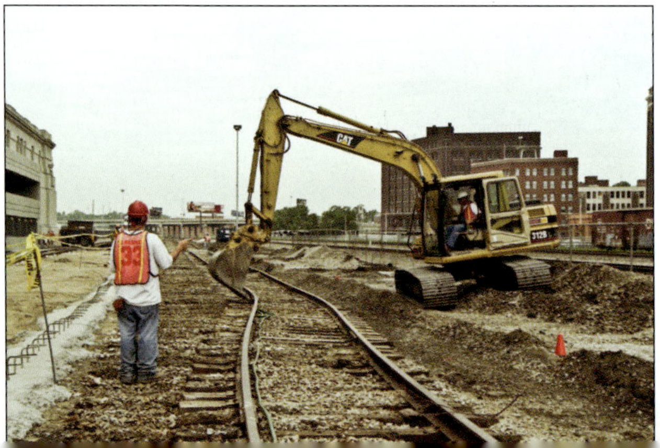

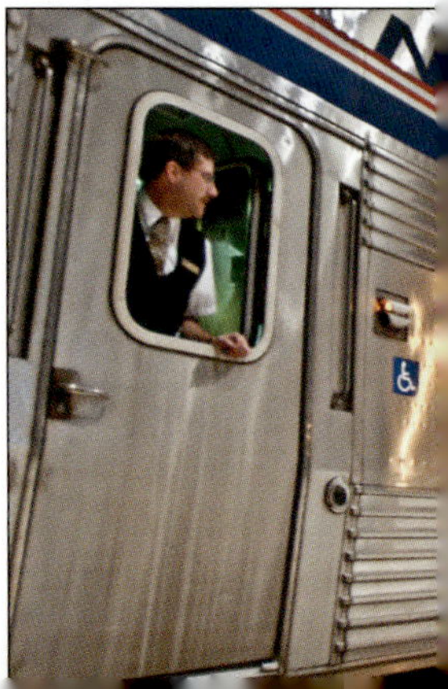

Chapter 4
The Station's Rebirth

As the new millennium began in 2000, Union Station was once again Kansas City's gathering place. In the first year after its reopening, more than one million people visited the station to marvel at the refurbished building, visit its shops and restaurants and attend private parties, wedding receptions, gala dinners, charity fundraisers and many other events.

Halfway through the first year, access to the station improved with the opening of a striking, glass-enclosed skywalk called The Link, which connected the station to Crown Center and the Westin Hotel. The curving, 900-foot skywalk created a convenient all-weather route for tourists and local residents to reach Union Station's offerings. In 2002, Amtrak agreed to return passenger service to Union Station for the first time since 1985, as plans were announced for a new $5 million train station.

But for all the goodwill surrounding the station's rebirth, its central attraction – Science City – failed to draw as many people as predicted, and Union Station operated at a $9.5 million deficit in 2000, its first full year in operation. Deficits deepened over the next few years amid evidence that Science City did not draw enough interest beyond the 5 to 9 age group. In early 2005, Sci-

Continued on page 74

Amtrak Returns, Left – *Finished and bright and shiny, the new $4.5 million Amtrak facility officially opened Dec. 17, 2002, but had been operating a week before. As of 2014, six trains operated out of Union Station.*

Bottom Row, Left to Right – *Work was progressing rapidly on the Amtrak boarding platform, or arcade, when this photo was taken from a bucket lift. The roof has been installed over the walkway from the ticketing/waiting room and tracks are in place.*

To accommodate the configuration of the new boarding platform, tracks were moved and repositioned.

The Superliner cars of the Southwest Chief are an impressive sight as they arrive and depart.

The late Carolyn and Pete McMasters were enthusiastic supporters of Amtrak and Union Station. Pete bought the last ticket sold when Amtrak left the station in December of 1985 – a $4.78 round trip to Independence. But it was not for a train ride. They just wanted to have the last ticket as a memento. It is now on display in the station's KC Rail Experience. The bench the McMasters are sitting on is one of three from the station's North Waiting Room that were rescued from a Grain Valley barn, refurbished and returned to Union Station's new Amtrak waiting room.

The Amtrak ticketing/waiting room is located on the northeast corner of the station just off the Grand Hall.

Bloch Fountain, Top – *The Bloch Fountain is strategically located in the center of Pershing Road, flanked by the World War I Liberty Memorial and Museum on the south and Union Station on the north.*

Above – *Hundreds of supports were placed for the Henry Wollman Bloch Memorial Fountain black granite ellipse. The water display employs 232 jets arranged in three concentric rings. The well-known WET Design firm conceived and designed the fountain.*

Right – *Henry Bloch, co-founder with his brother Richard (not shown) of the H&R Block Company, turned a ceremonial valve Sept. 25, 2001, officially adding the fountain to Kansas City's already world-famous water display portfolio. The opening ceremonies had originally been scheduled for Sept. 12, 2001, but were postponed to the later date because of the tragic events of 9-11. The fountain was a gift to the city by the Marion and Henry Bloch Family Foundation in honor of the retiring Henry Bloch.*

The Station's Rebirth 67

The Link, Above & Left – *"This is harder than going to the moon!"* proclaimed Andy Scott. He was referring to the many municipal entities that needed to approve of and be on board with the construction of The Link, the elevated, climate-controlled walkway connecting Union Station with Crown Center. At the outcome, all were in agreement and some months after the station reopened in 1999, The Link debuted and has been an overwhelming success with locals and tourists alike.

The Kansas City Ballet, Top Left – *Located on the far west end of the Union Station property, the ancient powerhouse provided electricity for the station and for a number of surrounding buildings. Before the restoration, it was a mass of rusting, twisted beams and remnants of machines from the early 1900s.*

Top Right – *Young ballerinas practiced in the renovated space under the watchful eye of the artistic director of the Kansas City Ballet Devon Carney. The little girls would take on the persona of baby flamingos in the Ballet's fall 2014 production of "Alice (In Wonderland)."*

Above – *The former Union Station powerhouse is now called The Todd Bolender Center for Dance and Creativity. The renovated building became the home of the Kansas City Ballet in August of 2011.*

Right – *A skylight was installed where the 150'-tall smoke stack for the power generating station once stood. The tall space now provides an excellent spot to judge color and drape costumes, as well as allows a soft, calming light from above. Jessica Kelly, left, electronic media coordinator and Linda Martin, director, community program, compared dresses.*

The Michael R. Haverty Freight House Bridge And Dedication – *The tale of this classic truss railroad bridge begins with its construction in 1892. It was build to connect the Consolidated Terminal Railway, a Kansas City Southern predecessor, with the East and West Bottoms. Moving the two sections of the three-section span was a monumental undertaking, and was documented by the History Channel on "Mega Movers." It connects the station with the Crossroads and the Freight House restaurants. J.E. Dunn Construction was the general contractor on the bridge installation. In June, 2012 it was renamed The Michael R. Haverty Freight House Bridge in honor of his support and dedication to Union Station.* **Photo at Right –** *George Guastello, Union Station president and CEO, from left, Michael Haverty, outgoing Union Station Board Chairman and Bob Regnier, incoming Board Chairman, posed for photos at the dedication.*

The Kansas City Area Development Council and the Greater Kansas City Chamber of Commerce – *Two high-profile tenants that have relocated to Union Station are the KCADC, or Kansas City Area Development Council, top and the Greater Kansas City Chamber of Commerce, above and right.*

National Archives – The old Adams Express Freight building on the west side of the main Union Station building now houses the Kansas City field location wing of the National Archives. Nestled between the United States Postal Service and Kansas City Ballet, the Archives occupies more than 35,000 square feet of restored space. The facility is open to the public for research projects and contains thousands of paper documents and artifacts. But there is also artwork, like this wall-sized painting, "Pony Express" by Edward "Buk" Ulreich. There is also an area for periodically changing exhibits that display artifacts from the collection. The Archives opened to the public in its new space in May of 2009.

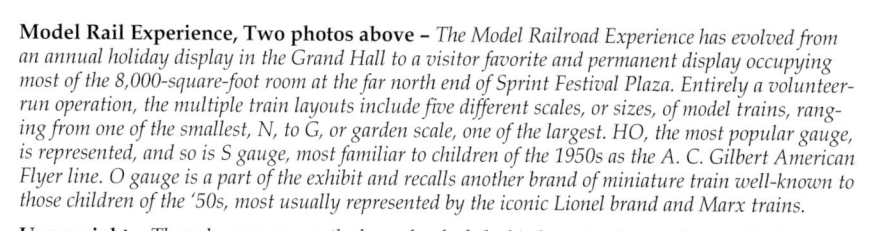

Model Rail Experience, Two photos above – *The Model Railroad Experience has evolved from an annual holiday display in the Grand Hall to a visitor favorite and permanent display occupying most of the 8,000-square-foot room at the far north end of Sprint Festival Plaza. Entirely a volunteer-run operation, the multiple train layouts include five different scales, or sizes, of model trains, ranging from one of the smallest, N, to G, or garden scale, one of the largest. HO, the most popular gauge, is represented, and so is S gauge, most familiar to children of the 1950s as the A. C. Gilbert American Flyer line. O gauge is a part of the exhibit and recalls another brand of miniature train well-known to those children of the '50s, most usually represented by the iconic Lionel brand and Marx trains.*

Upper right – *The subway scene on the lower level of the big layout is designed especially for tots.*

Lower Right – *Isabel Fowler and Kaiden Canales, Children of Union Station employees, enjoyed the interactive toy train layout for younger children.*

The Station's Rebirth   73

The USPS, Left & Below – *The United States Postal Service main customer facility in Kansas City had been located for about 70 years in a classic building constructed for the post office and located almost directly across Pershing Road from Union Station. The USPS and the station had a physical connection: A tunnel ran under Pershing, uphill from C level to the basement of the post office. Mail was shuttled back and forth between the two buildings in carts via the tunnel. Railway Post Office cars, eliminated in the 1970s, were loaded and unloaded at the station. But there came a point when the enormous old building was more space than the USPS needed. An agreement was reached between the USPS and the station: The old REA (Railway Express Agency) building immediately to the west of the station would house the processing facilities of the postal service, and the customer retail counter would be inside the main building on the Grand Hall level. The USPS board of governors announced funding approval in February of 2004, and the postal service moved to its new quarters April 1~3, 2005. This was a significant step forward in helping solve the station's financial woes of the early 2000s.*

Continued from page 65

ence City replaced a child-oriented dinosaur bone dig with DinoLab, where visitors could watch experts assemble a skeletal model of a 140-million-year-old, 60-foot-long dinosaur named Lyle. Lab workers patched and cleaned original bones to create models for the skeleton. DinoLab helped stabilize attendance at Science City through the rest of the decade.

In 2004, the station bought antique rail cars from a Milwaukee collector to put on display in the KC Rail Experience. The train cars gave visitors a glimpse of the golden

Continued on page 76

Dinos, Above & Right – *A dinosaur exhibit in 2010 was announced with a life-sized replica that loomed menacingly from behind the Union Station marquee. Inside Science City resides a permanent dinosaur replica.*

KC Rail Experience, Above & Left – *The KC Rail Experience is an interactive, story-telling exhibit that traces the history and significance of railroads to America, to the region and to Kansas City. A locomotive simulator donated by BNSF Railway has an authentic cab, complete with all the controls used by engineers. Much of the story is told by "ghost" figures from Union Station's past, who speak as visitors approach them. From station architect Jarvis Hunt, to an engineer, to a Harvey Girl and a World War II sailor, visitors learn the history from the people who were there.*

Classic Cars – *Dozens of beautifully restored automobiles were displayed at Union Station in 2004.*

Continued from page 74

age of rail travel. In 2006, Kansas City Southern moved a former train bridge to Union Station. It became an overhead walkway to the Freight House district to the north, which evolved into the tony Crossroads Arts District. In 2008, the 20,000 square foot Bank of America exhibit gallery opened to host major traveling exhibits, such as Bodies Revealed, Dinosaurs Unearthed, Princess Diana and Titanic. The exhibits brought hundreds of thousands of visitors to the station.

All of the improvements at Union Station reduced annual deficits to about $1 million by 2008, but continued losses loomed because revenue could not keep pace with hefty expenses. Just keeping the giant station heated, cooled and maintained cost $2.5 million annually. The Kansas City Council rebuffed efforts to raise property taxes to help the station survive. As the 10th anniversary of its reopening neared, there was even some talk about closing the insolvent station.

In December 2008, the station board of directors hired a new chief executive – George Guastello, a Kansas City native who was previously the CEO of the American Royal. Ironically, as the recession gripped the country in 2009, Union Station began its turnaround. Guastello and the board, with guidance from business solutions company DST Systems of Kansas City, decided to take a hard look at how every dime was spent at Union Station. They concluded that Union Station, a non-profit corporation, was involved in too many parts of the building's operation – from running restaurants and shops to doing the nightly cleaning. "We were doing everything for everybody." Guastello said. "It wasn't run like a business."

Guastello and Jerry Baber, Chief Financial Officer, outsourced as much of the Union Station operation as possible, which cut costs and payroll. They also decided in 2010 that Union Station could produce a lot more revenue from office development. Leasing had already been a key source of some income, such as the move of the U.S. Postal Service to Union Station in 2005. The station board targeted two high-profile civic organizations as new tenants – the Greater Kansas City Chamber of Commerce and the Kansas City Area Development Council. Both agreed to move in, and later the station added Kansas City Area Life Sciences, the Kansas City Election Board and professional development offices of the University of Missouri-Kansas City, as well as several

Continued on page 80

The Olympic Torch, Above – *The Olympic Torch heralding the start of the 2002 Winter Olympics at Rice-Eccles Stadium in Salt Lake City passed through Kansas City and Union Station Jan. 9, 2002. It was a 65-day run in America after its traditional start in Athens, Greece, in Dec. of 2001.*

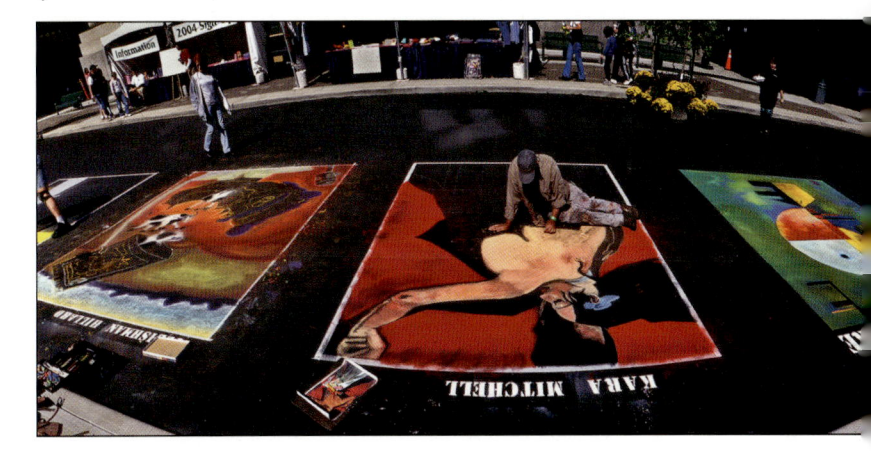

Sidewalk Art 2003, Above – *Sidewalk art is an annual Kansas City event. In 2003, it was staged at Union Station.*

Race for the Cure, Left & Below – *The annual Race for the Cure is one of the two largest events that happen at Union Station, along with the Celebration at the Station. The Cure draws 25,000 runners, many of them breast cancer survivors.*

Royal Wedding Watch Party, Top & Above – *More than 3,500 people, most of them women, crowded into Sprint Festival Plaza before 4:30 a.m. Apr. 29, 2011, to be part of the Royal Wedding Watch Party. They joined a virtual global village that was enthralled with the uniting of England's Prince William, Duke of Cambridge, and Catherine Middleton. Large view screens at the north end of the Plaza captured every moment. Many who attended were appropriately dressed for a royal wedding.*

Center right – *Coinciding with the party was the Princess Diana exhibit at Union Station. Her wedding dress was one of the highlights of the display.*

Kansas City Fashion Week, Above & Left – *Teisha Marie Barber, with the puppy, is the president of Kansas City Fashion Week and these photos are from the first time that the event was at Union Station, the Fall of 2013. Many of Kansas City's top designers and boutiques were represented. Erin Page Designs showed a fabulous line of colorful, outsized jewelry, perfectly set off against white, floor-length dresses on tall models of almost the same height.*

Weddings, Below & Lower Left – *Union Station has been a popular location for nuptuials of all faiths and denominations. Represented here in the Sprint Festival Plaza are a Hindu wedding and a Christian wedding.*

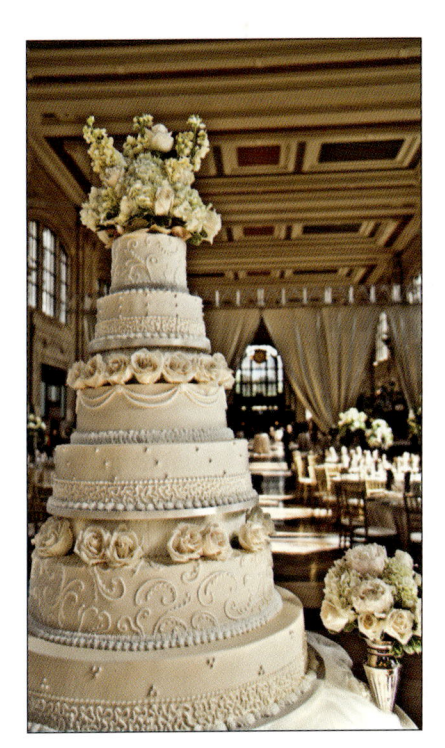

Continued from page 76

private businesses.

In the end, Union Station found economic survival by marketing its prestige to potential tenants. "If you could have one address for your business or organization what would it be?" Guastello said. "The biggest, most beloved monument in Kansas City." After years of deficits, Union Station enjoyed four straight years of seven-digit cash surpluses as it observed its 100th anniversary in 2014. "And we have done it on our own – with no dedicated tax revenue," Guastello said, adding that private donations and funding remain impor-

Continued on page 82

Dead Sea Scrolls, Above & Right – *Another blockbuster exhibit at Union Station was the Dead Sea Scrolls that showed from Feb. 8~May 13, 2007. Thousands upon thousands of guests visited the elaborate set and viewed the centuries-old documents, some of the earliest remaining artifacts in Judeo-Christian history. A replica depicting how one of the caves might have looked where the Scrolls were discovered was constructed and positioned under the clock. On opening night, a live camel with handler set the stage for visitors even before patrons entered the station.*

Right – *Isabel Fowler and Kaiden Canales, Children of Union Station employees, enjoyed the interactive toy train layout for younger children.*

Pirates, Top – *The information booth in the Grand Hall was decorated with Real Pirates promotions and was a glowing spectacle in early morning light.*

Above – *Looking for all the world like real pirates from another century, interactors performed rousing seafaring songs at the exhibit's opening night.*

Center Left & Below Left – *Inside the exhibit were many genuine artifacts from an actual pirate ship, a mock-up, a ship itself and lots of facts about the art of pirating.*

Continued from page 80
tant to the station.

In 2011, the station began taking its marquee attraction to a new level when Science City received $1.25 million from Burns & McDonnell to fund new exhibits and a Battle of the Brains contest. Students in grades K-12 from across the Kansas City region compete in Battle of the Brains to create exhibits at Science City that demonstrate skills in science, technology, engineering and math, or STEM. The initial winning entry, designed by students at Olathe North High School, became The Science of Energy, which lets visitors actively capture and transfer body energy and encourages them to explore global energy issues.

In 2012, Science City opened a new Science on a Sphere exhibit that projects images and programs about space, earth sciences, the weather and other topics on a giant sphere. In early 2013, the station reopened the renovated Regnier Extreme Screen Theater to show 3-D nature films and first-run movies on the largest screen in the region. The screen can also live-stream special presentations or conferences. Special traveling exhibits continued to shine at Union Station, such as Real Pirates in 2013, which drew more than 70,000 visitors. In 2014, Union Station became the North American premier site for The Discovery of King Tut, a famed traveling collection of dazzling artifacts from the tomb of the teenage king of ancient Egypt.

In its 100th year, Union Station is, in a sense, back at its beginning as a union of interests brought together in one place. Just as railroads came together to form the station, 100 years later the station is a union of culture, business, dining, entertainment, education, travel, commerce and history. "It's a city within a city," Guastello said. "It is exactly how Jarvis Hunt designed it."

King Tut – *The North American premier of the Discovery of King Tut exhibit was presented at Union Station the summer and early fall of 2014. Tutankhamen, the boy king of Egypt, was buried with a treasure trove of artifacts in his tomb, hundreds of which were meticulously reproduced for this stunning exhibit.*

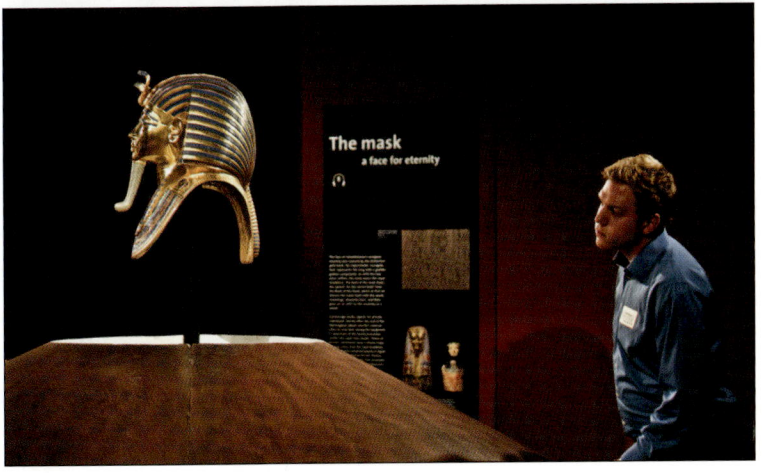

The Station's Rebirth 83

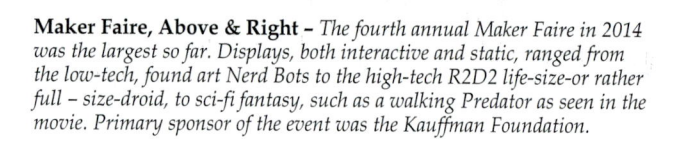

Maker Faire, Above & Right – *The fourth annual Maker Faire in 2014 was the largest so far. Displays, both interactive and static, ranged from the low-tech, found art Nerd Bots to the high-tech R2D2 life-size-or rather full – size-droid, to sci-fi fantasy, such as a walking Predator as seen in the movie. Primary sponsor of the event was the Kauffman Foundation.*

Titanic, Above & Left – *The Titanic mystique continues more than 100 years after the vessel sank in the frigid North Atlantic, killing more than 1,500 people on that early morning of Apr. 15, 1912. Two different Titanic exhibits visited Union Station after the restoration. At the opening of the most recent traveling exhibit on March 2, 2012, a string quartet played the same pieces as did the musicians on board the fated ship.*

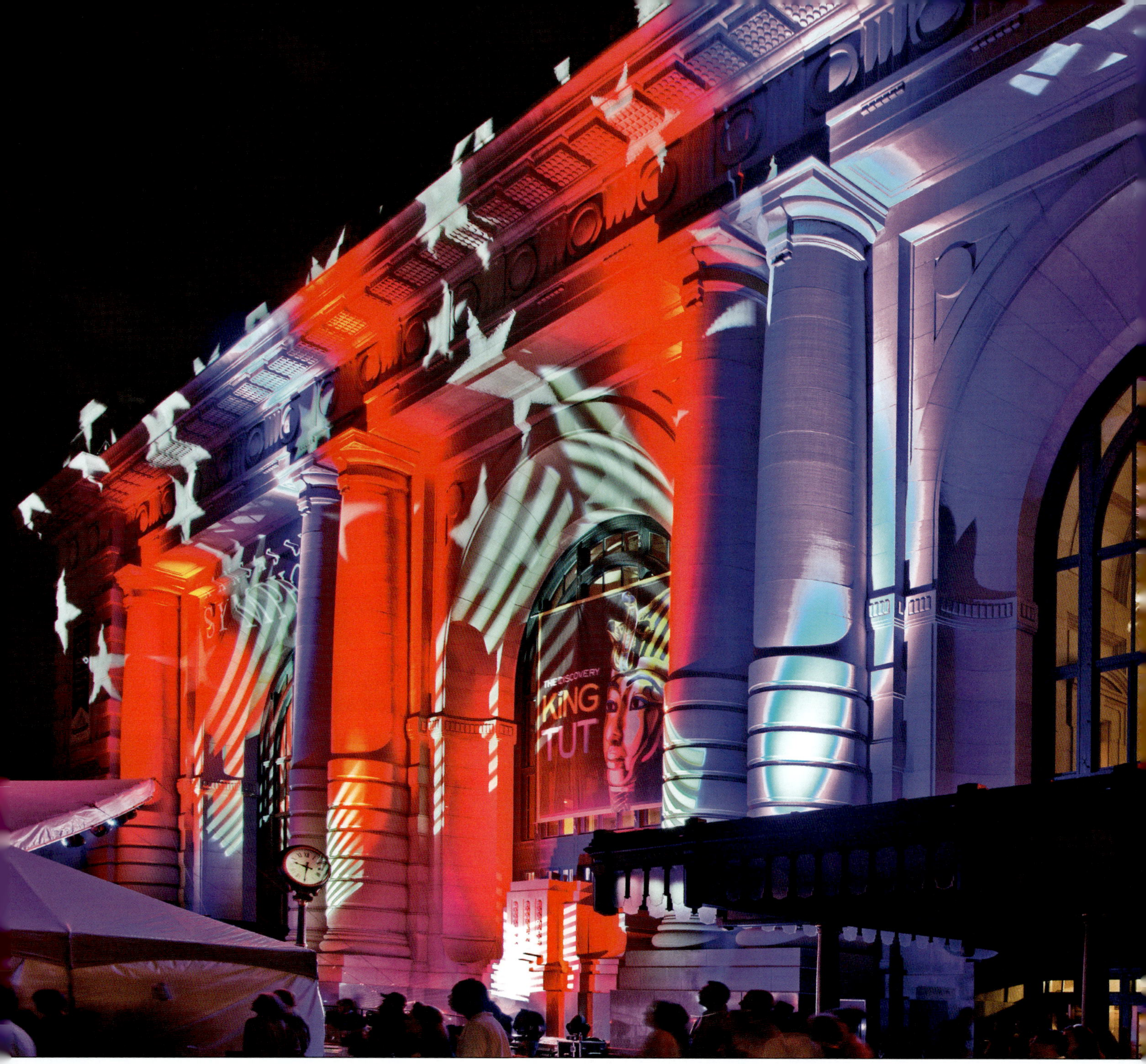
KING
TUT

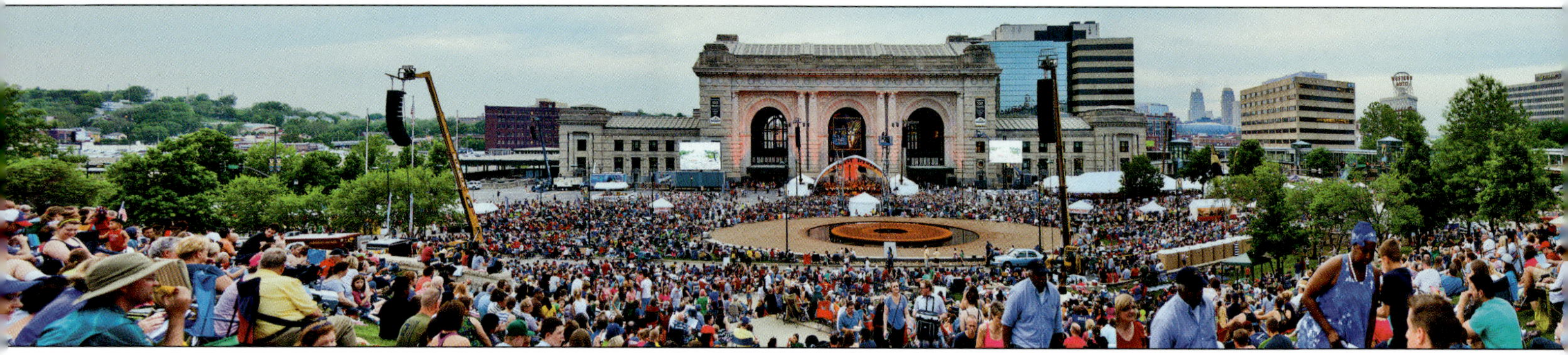

The Station's Rebirth   87

Celebration at the Station, Top Left – *Magical, patriotic colors splashed across the station's front as a salute to men and women who have served and who are serving in America's armed forces.*

Far Left – *An estimated 40,000 turned out for this 12th annual Celebration at the Station Sunday, May 25, 2014.*

Left – *The station and the band shell that sheltered the Kansas City Symphony were bathed in a continually changing, wildly colorful light show.*

Chapter 5
The Future of Union Station

The 100th anniversary of Union Station in 2014 arrived at a high point in the landmark's vaunted history. After years of financial struggles since it reopened in 1999, the station had four straight years of profitability.

Entering its second century, Union Station faced a bright but still demanding future.

"It's going to take a lot of work, all the time," said Bob Regnier, chairman of the Union Station Board of Directors as the station observed its 100th anniversary. "The key is to always make it an interesting place. Keep it on everybody's list of places to go."

Union Station found financial viability by supporting its entertainment and educational venues with revenue from leased office space. The station became the address of the Greater Kansas City Chamber of Commerce and other organizations and businesses, creating revenue to pay the bills and to save for the years ahead.

"We are starting to invest in the future," Regnier said.

An early project in the station's second century will be the addition of a car and pedestrian bridge from the third level of the parking garage to the west side of Union Station, providing direct access to the station's main level.

"Union Station is the front door of Kansas City and our focus has to be on customer service," said George Guastello, the station's chief executive. "Union Station will always evolve to meet the needs of people at the time."

The area between the parking garage and planetarium is to become an events plaza, with shaded seating, garden areas, a stage and a display of historic rail cars. It will also have a new connection to the Michael R. Haverty Bridge to the Crossroads and Freight House districts, tying those popular areas more closely to Union Station.

Also on the drawing boards as the station turned 100 was a 2,800-square-foot, indoor-outdoor structure next to the renovated Gottlieb Planetarium, with seating for up to 120 people. School groups could use the space, which would also accommodate receptions and pre-event gatherings.

Other proposals for the station include an upgraded lobby allowing guests to move between Science City and theater attractions without leaving the science center. A new futuristic "space portal" is proposed linking Science City to the planetarium and the renovated 3D Regnier Extreme Screen Theater.

In a more practical sense, Union Station is an old building and will continue to need repairs, such as a new roof 15 or so years into the station's second century, Regnier said. For that project and others, the station's board is setting aside money for a long-range capital improvement plan, he said.

As science and theater attractions continue to improve, the station will remain committed to drawing major exhibits, building upon the successes of shows such as The Discovery of King Tut in 2014, Regnier said.

"We want to have two really solid exhibits every year – one for spring and summer and one for fall and winter, including the holiday season," Regnier said.

Union Station, with its vast Grand Hall and north wing, will remain a major draw for galas, dinners, weddings, private parties and a wide range of public and corporate events.

"It's a beautiful building and we want to leverage that," Regnier said.

Restaurants and retail stores are expected to continue to be important players in the everyday life of Union Station. So will be the roots of Union Station's existence – rail travel.

"What is amazing is that every day someone is getting on or off a train at Union Station, just as they did years ago," Guastello said. "People are dining at the station every day and you never know when you might see the mayor or a con-

Continued on page 90

Continued from page 89

gressman walking the hall. You are seeing business leaders and you are seeing diversity. You sit under the big clock and you will not believe how many people are coming and going."

Union Station was one of the largest train stations in the United States when it opened in 1914, and rail travel holds a key to its future, said Michael R. Haverty, a longtime member of the station's board of directors and the former CEO of Kansas City Southern.

Haverty said Union Station can serve as the center of a proposed light rail and streetcar network in Kansas City, to go along with existing Amtrak service to cities across America.

"I am convinced that at some point in time

Union Station is going to again be a rail and transportation hub," Haverty said. "The most successful stations in the United States – such as in Washington, Los Angeles and Denver – have trains running at the stations all the time. They put people in the building and those people are spending money."

Union Station's growth as a center for transportation, entertainment, culture, learning and business has made it the face of Kansas City, Haverty said.

"Almost every picture you see promoting Kansas City on a national basis has Union Station in it," Haverty said. "It really has become Kansas City's icon and it continues to get better and better."

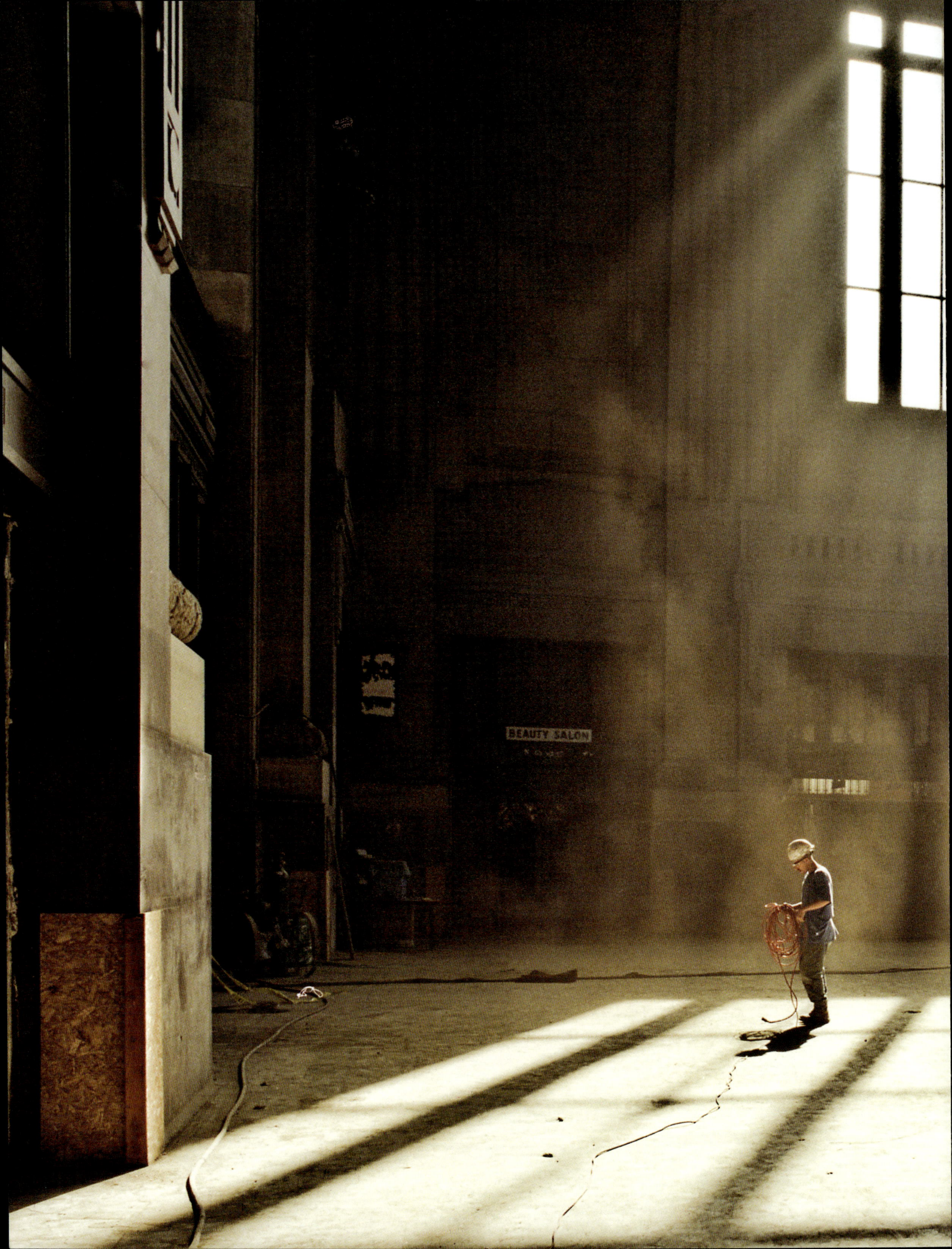
BEAUTY SALON

GALLERY

This final chapter includes a collection of favorite Union Station vignettes and images compiled by Union Station photographer Roy Inman during his 20-year documentation of the historic depot. There are pictures of the restoration, illustrated experiences, visiting trains and photos reflecting the beauty of the station over the seasons.

Surrounded By Beam Particles – *Light is both a beam and particles. When some sort of diffusion interrupts those light beams, the particles become visible. At the beginning of the restoration, there was occasional dust in the station that created a perfect backdrop for striking photographs.*

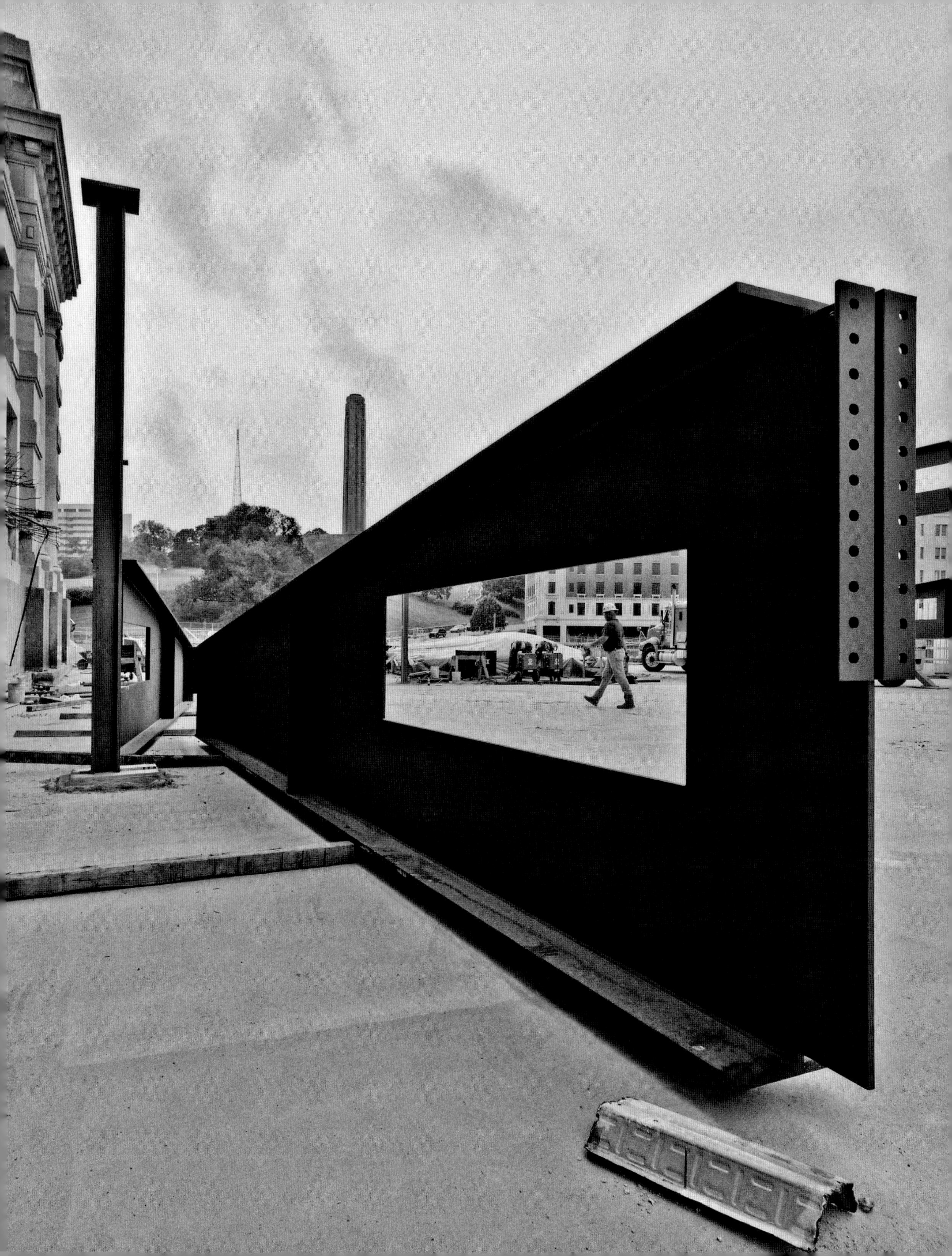

Carriage Pavilion Beam, Opposite – *Large beams awaited installation during the reconstruction of the Carriage Pavilion.*

I Miss Life, Above – *Over the decades, there have been rumors of a mentally-impaired man who lived in Union Station in the dank underground, far away from the hustle and bustle of the throngs upstairs. Jim Lehrer even wrote a novel based on the legend. This cryptic marking was probably left by a prankster sometime during the restoration and not by the mysterious hermit. But the legend is that he did leave some scribblings behind…*

Round Window Wash, Left – *The last few weeks and days were hectic prior to the re-opening of the station in 1999. Everything had to be spic and span, including the two classic round windows on the front of the building.*

Native American Sculpture Install, Right – *Two plaster likenesses of Native Americans reside above the fireplace on the third floor, east side of Union Station. The story is that they represent the chiefs from whom the land was purchased lo those many years ago. As the restoration progressed, the heads were removed to prevent damage, but one morning a head was missing. As is usual in such cases, no one knew anything. The supervisor called a meeting with all the workers, and he informed the gathering that if the chief's countenance was not in his office by tomorrow morning, all were fired. Next morning, a worker showed up with the sculpture, and it was damaged. As good fortune would have it, a restorer at the Nelson Atkins Museum was able to make it as new. Previous photographs of the undamaged original taken by Roy Inman helped guide the process.*

Laying House Tracks, Below – *Rail fans were excited when new house tracks were run from a main line behind the station. And in a recreation of a scene from yesteryear, the tracks were laid by hand, by Gandydancers – that's the term used to describe the men who used to do that sort of thing. The process is rare these days because sophisticated machines do most of the difficult and dangerous work.*

Window Weed, Above – *It began as a tiny, barely-noticed sprout. But it grew taller in this most unlikely of places – a gable at the second floor of Union Station. Life will find a way, and this little weed did. Construction workers helped it along by giving it plant food and regular watering. In the fullness of time, the brave spec of life, improbably existing in a slit between marble slabs, grew to nearly three feet in height. The grand reopening of the station drew near, and one day the supervisor casually told one of the workmen to "get up there and remove it." The worker refused. So did all the rest. Someone suggested that Roy Inman's assistant that day, Kathy Wismer, go up on a lift and do the deed. THAT did not fly. This was a life, some would say an insignificant plant life but one that had survived against all odds, not unlike the Union Station. But it just would not do for a weed to be in full view on the front of a $260 million newly recreated station. At length the supervisor was now frustrated and angry. He took aside one of the workers and ordered him to remove the weed. The worker reluctantly agreed, but said he would not do it in front of the other men. He would terminate the life under cover of darkness. So it was that one moonless night in November just before the reopening, a courageous little weed met its fate. But its memory lives on in this photograph.*

Historic Floors, Left – *More than 400 pairs of boots tramped through Union Station during the restoration. To better protect the relatively soft marble underfoot, hundreds of square feet of thick plywood was installed. A large banner reminded everyone.*

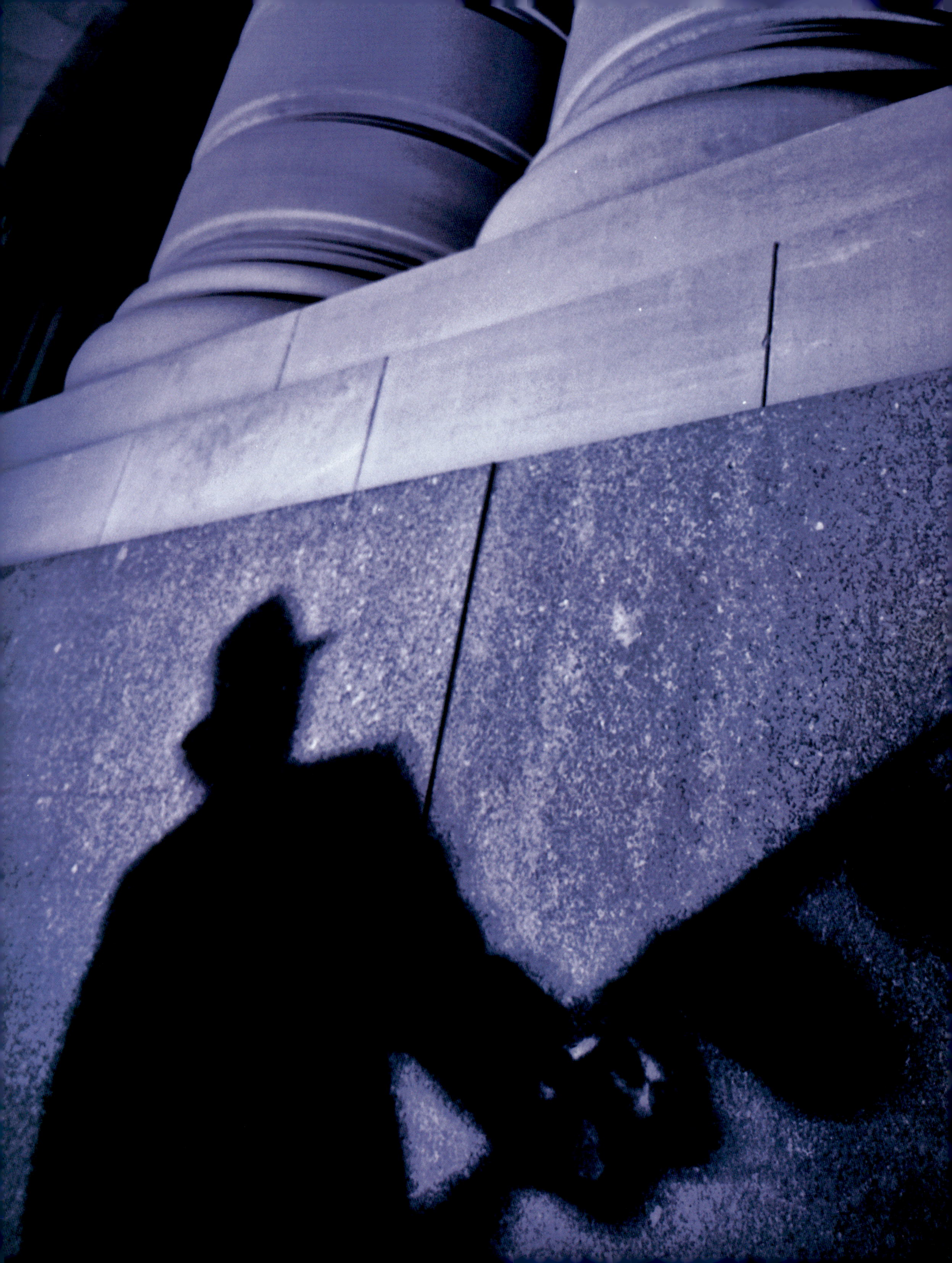

Union Station Massacre, Left & Above – *Convicted train and bank robber Frank Nash had escaped from the Federal Penitentiary in Leavenworth in October of 1930. He eluded capture for nearly three years, and was finally apprehended in Hot Springs, Ark. With Nash in tow, the arresting lawmen traveled by train to Kansas City on June 17, 1933, but the next train to Leavenworth from Union Station was not for several hours. The lawmen figured it would be safer for all concerned to not sit around in the station awaiting the next departure. They would drive by motorcar to the prison, a fateful decision that would indirectly lead to the transformation of law enforcement in America. However, friends of Nash found out about the transfer and made plans to intercept the contingent at Union Station and free their buddy. They were well armed, and at least two carried Thompson sub-machine guns. Things did not go as planned. Four lawmen and Nash were killed during the resultant bloody shootout in broad daylight in front of the station. The incident stunned the nation and Congress. As a result, the FBI was given increased legal authority and the bureau's agents could all carry firearms. Before the Union Station Massacre, most had not been armed. There is some contention that the holes in the front wall of the station are not really bullet holes. But of course that begs the question: If the holes were not caused by bullets, then what created them?*

UNION PACIFIC 844

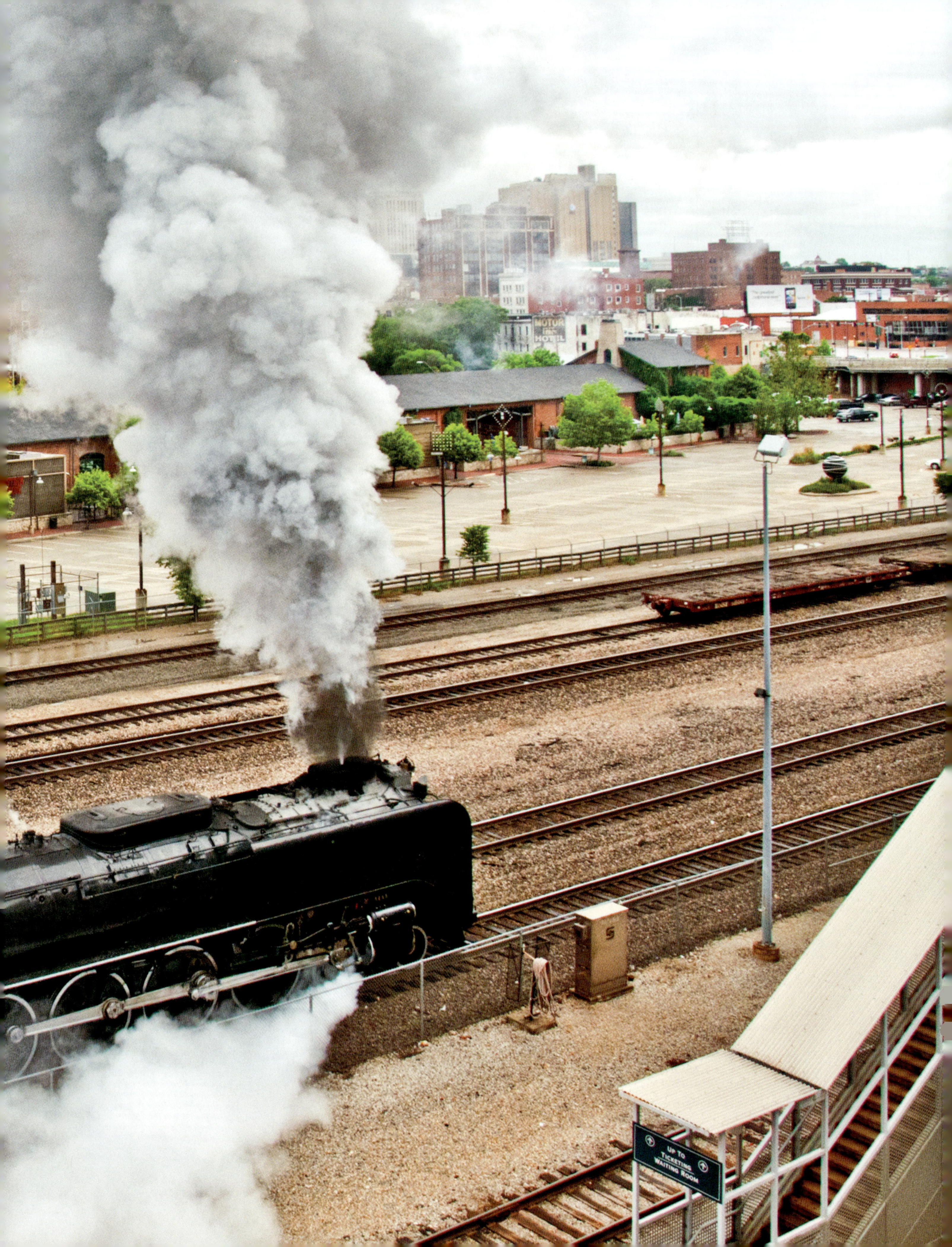
UP TO
TICKETING
WAITING ROOM

A Sign Of History, Above – On the wall of the west knuckle leading from the Grand Hall to Sprint Festival Plaza, there is a remnant from yesteryear that tells the tale of what Union Station was all about. The entire sign reads "To Departing Trains" with an arrow underneath, but the first part of the phrase is not really visible in a photograph. The same lettering is on the east side. The signs on both knuckles are visible with the naked eye, but one has to take a few minutes to figure out the right angle for viewing. I slightly digitally enhanced the letters to make them stand out a bit.

First 12 Railroads, Right – The colorful logos, or heralds, of the original twelve railroads that ran through Union Station are displayed against a background of one of the massive arched windows of the station in this poster created by Roy Inman. The Kansas City Southern, the hometown railroad, and the Union Pacific, based in Omaha, Neb., are the only two roads whose names remain intact. The Santa Fe lives on as part of the Burlington Northern Santa Fe.

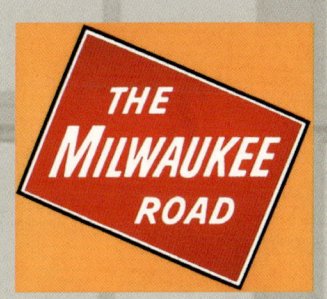

Railroads of Union Station Kansas City

Union Station at Kansas City, Missouri, is the second largest rail terminal still standing in the United States. Pennsylvania Station, before its destruction in 1963 was second largest. Grand Central Terminal in New York City remains the most massive. However, the baggage handling area of Union Station was bigger than any other because it had to be. An eastern depot typically ran one, two or three lines. Kansas City's Union Station hosted twelve Class 1 railroads shortly after its opening on October 30, 1914. These railroad heralds represent the original lines that operated passenger service out of Union Station. In the peak years during World War II, nearly 300 trains a day arrived and departed. The Kansas City Terminal Railway operated the facility.

Kansas City Terminal Railway

An EnterTrainment production© Union Station photograph Roy Inman©

Kansas City Southern Locomotives, Above & Right – *The Southern Belle locomotive has appeared in two different color schemes since the restoration of the station. The Brunswick Green livery, which records as almost black in photos, dates back several decades. Above – The bright yellow heritage livery with contrasting striping harkens back to the year 1940 when the Belle began service. This restored FP9 unit was donated by the Kansas City Southern and is a part of the KC Rail Museum at the station. A similar heritage color scheme has been adopted for the engines that lead the Southern Belle business train.*

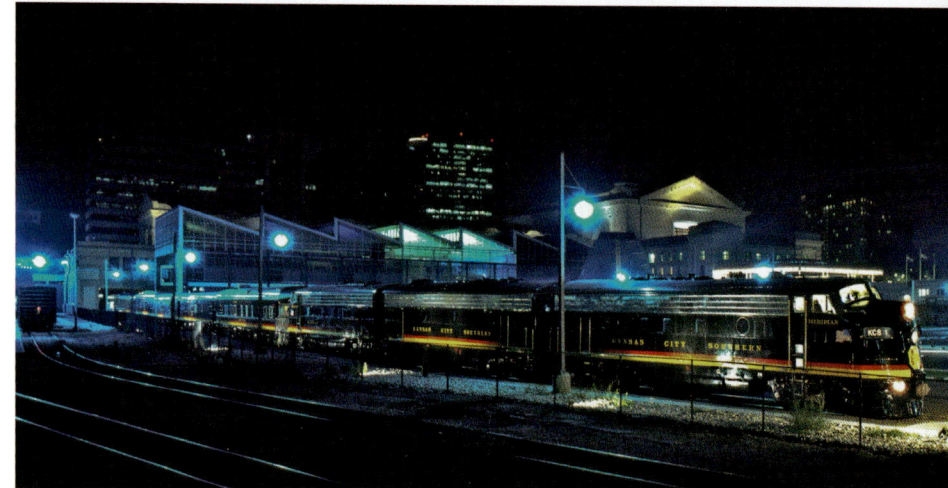

Milwaukee Road 261 And Skytop Lounge, Left & Below – *Friends of the 261 is a Minneapolis-based nonprofit that owns and maintains the former Milwaukee Road 4-8-4 steam locomotive, shown here on a visit to Union Station in 2005. Left – On that trip, the restored, iconic Skytop Lounge "Cedar Rapids" brought up the end of a consist of similarly-colored Milwaukee Road passenger cars. A famous industrial designer of the era, Brooks Stevens, created the fleet of striking passenger cars and the wildly popular observation car that entered service in 1948.*

The Holiday Express, Above – *The Holiday Express has become a beloved Kansas City holiday tradition. Each year since 2001, the festively-decorated, volunteer operated train has visited communities along the Kansas City Southern railroad's service area, from Shreveport, La., to St. Louis. Visitors of all ages may view and walk through the train at no charge. Inside are operating model train layouts, a large, sparkling toy display and Santa and Mrs. Claus, with their elf helpers. The Holiday Express also benefits communities. At each scheduled stop, the KCS Charitable Fund makes a contribution of gift cards to the local Salvation Army to provide warm clothing for children in need. Generous donations in the form of gift cards from KCS employees, vendors and friends have provided more than $1.2 million to the cause.*

The John S. Reed Locomotive, Right – *The family of the late John S. Reed, former chairman, president and CEO of the Santa Fe Railway donated this 1/8th scale locomotive to Union Station in 2008. It resides in a place of honor: under the clock.*

The Union Pacific Challenger, Far Right – *The Union Pacific Challenger 4-6-6-4 articulated steam locomotive has made several stops at Union Station, pulling a string of Impact Yellow UP passenger cars behind. Billed as the largest-operating steam locomotive in the world, the Challenger looked every bit the part on this day in 2004, dwarfing an awe-inspired boy.*

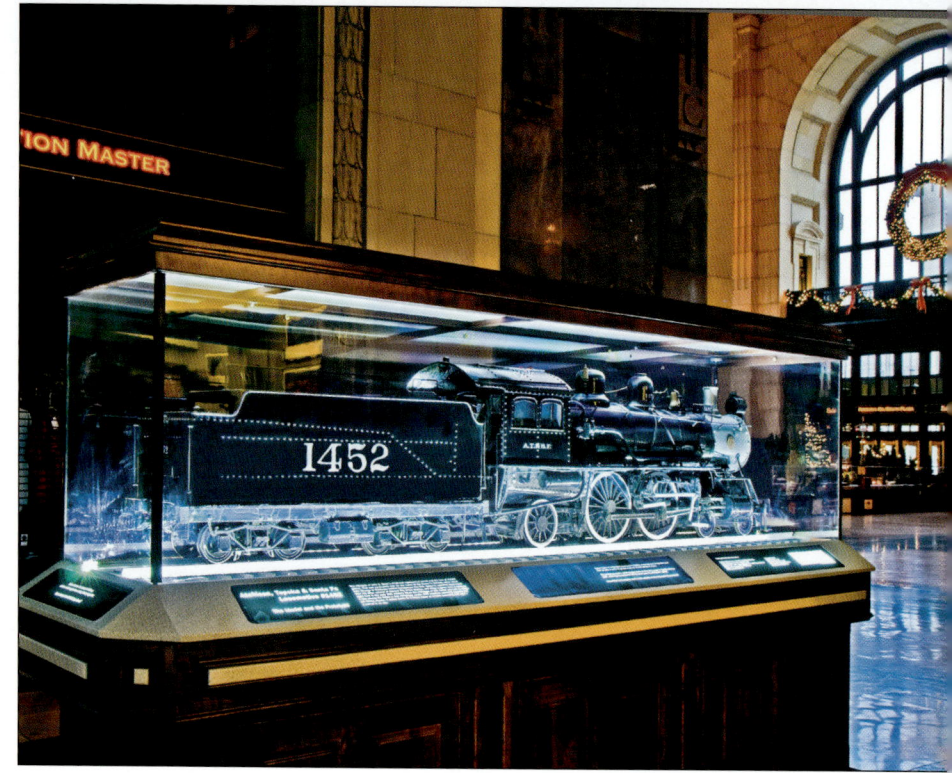

Union Pacific 844, Left – *The drive wheels of the Union Pacific 844 are more than six feet in diameter.*

Pullman Car, Below – *Railfan and Union Station supporter Armin Schannuth donned his conductor's uniform to help recreate a moment from the station's past. The Pullman car was on display at the station in 2007 but has since been relocated.*

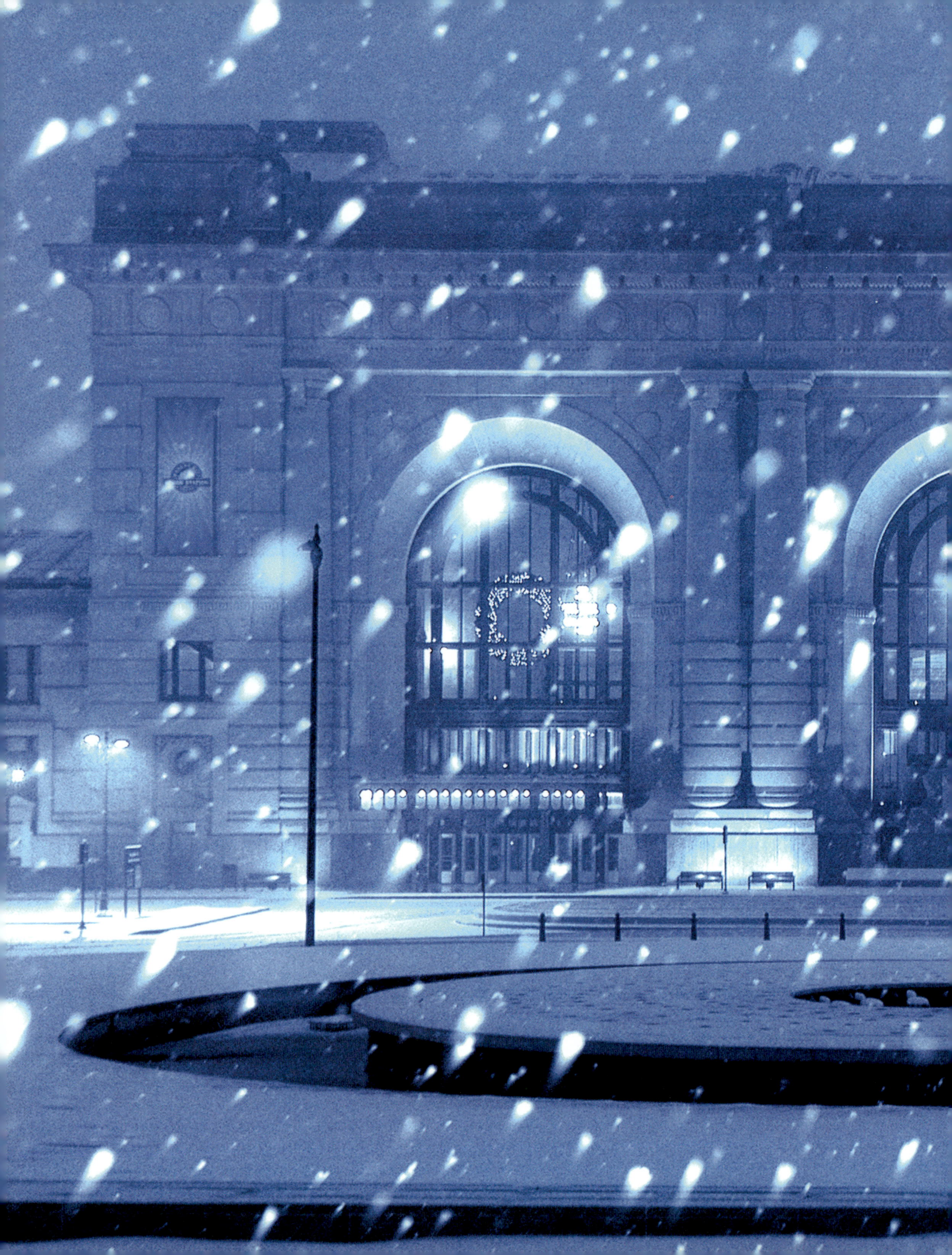

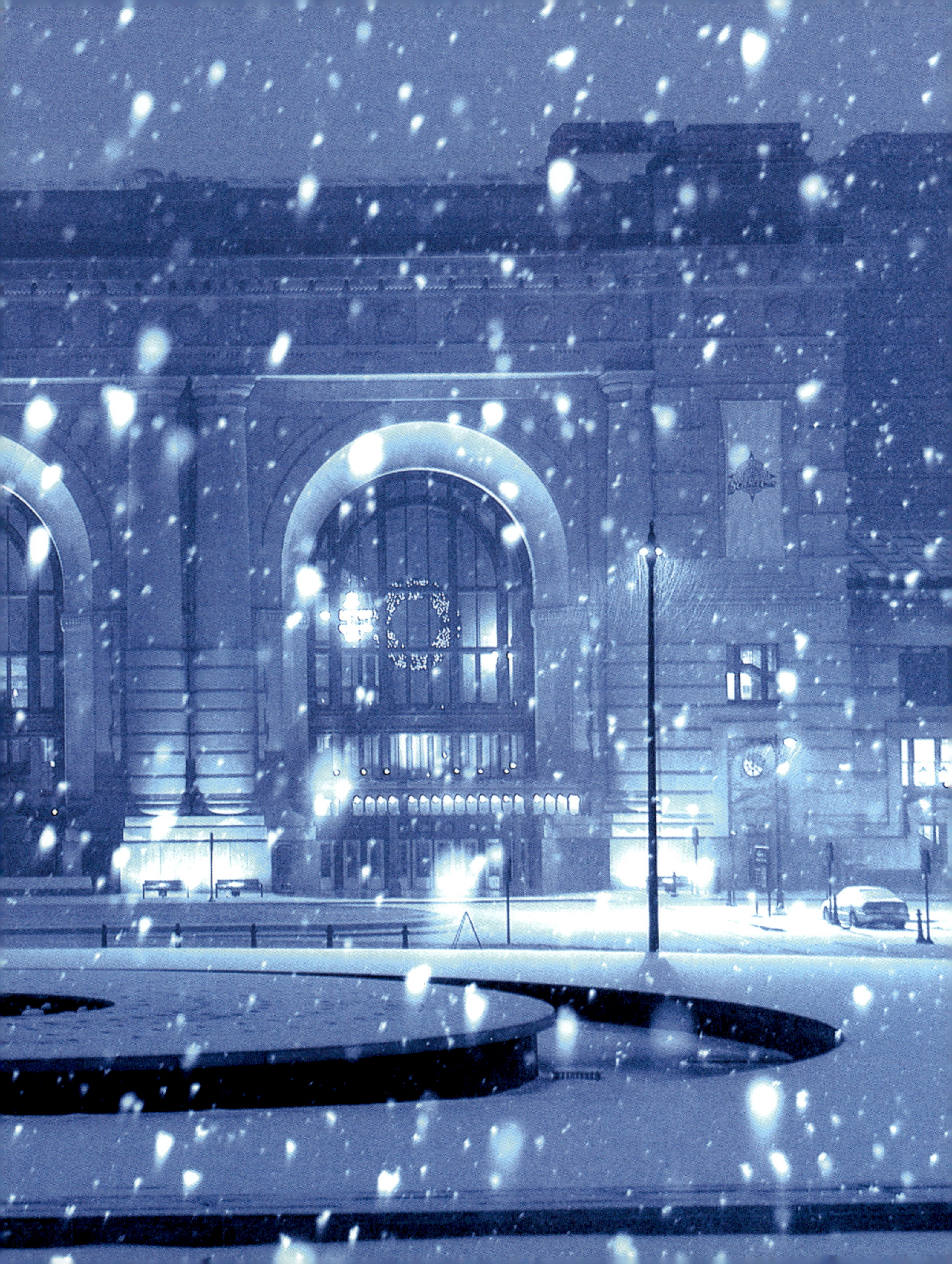

Dusk Station, Above – *Nearly two years of watching and waiting finally paid off: The photograph from Washington Park with leafless trees in the rain became a reality in April of 1999. And just in time, because construction on The Link began the next day, and this moody image of Union Station would never again be visible after the elevated walkway was finished.*

Windshield Rain, Right – *Union Station is a photo op almost anytime, but it is most appealing during a weather event, like a gentle spring rain.*

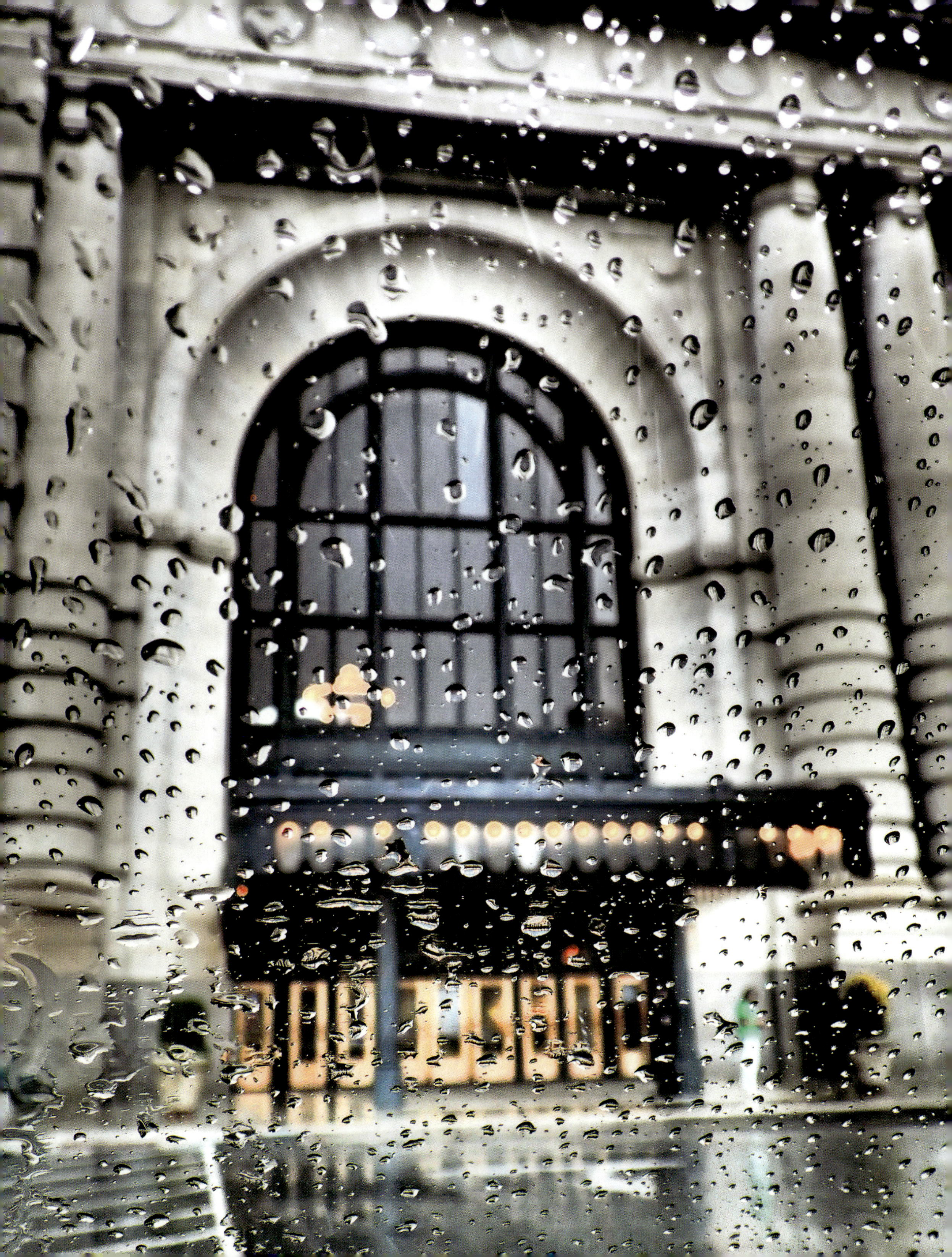

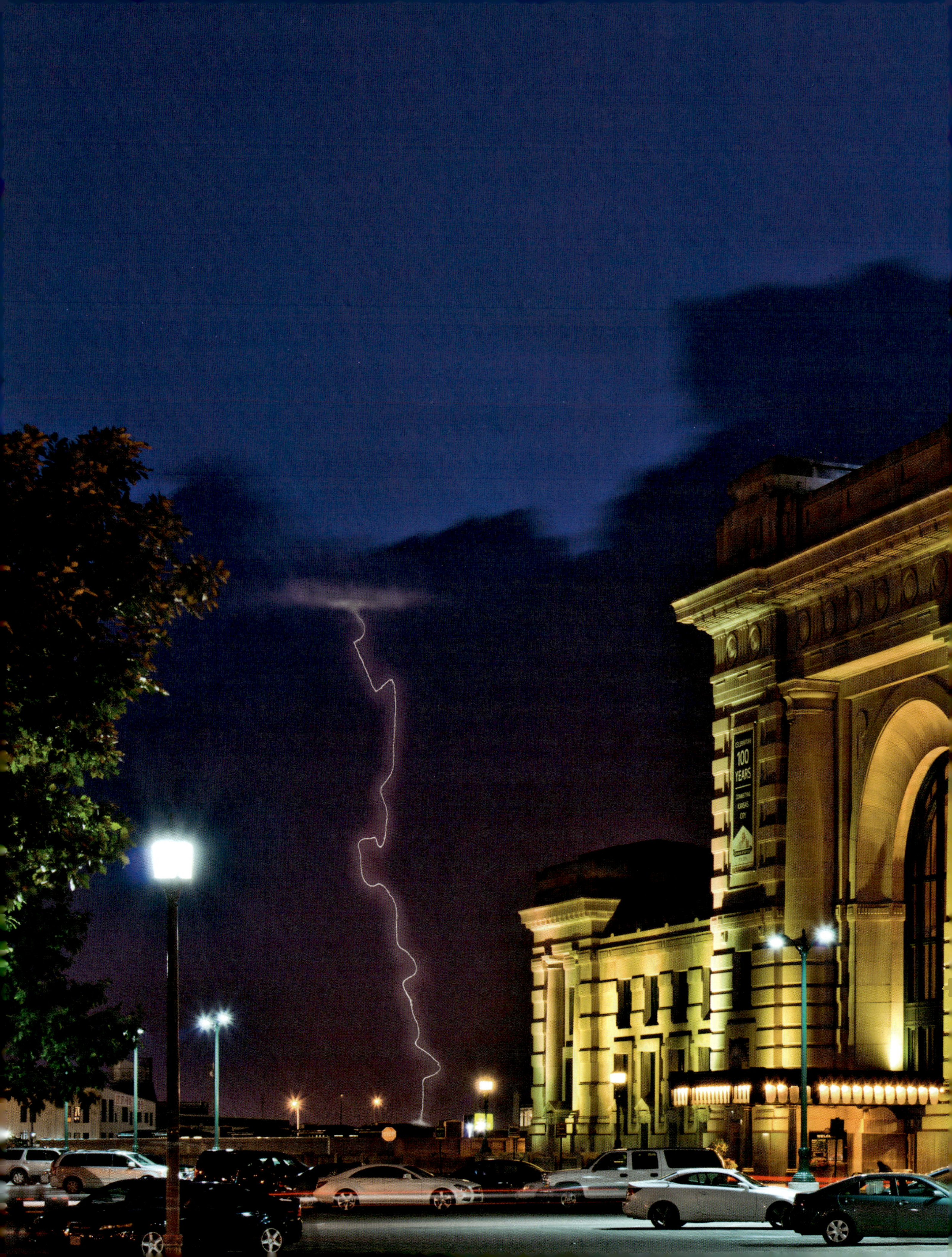
100
YEARS

CELEBRATING
100
YEARS
CONNECTING
KANSAS
CITY
UNION STATION
1914 - 2014
THE DISCOVERY
KING

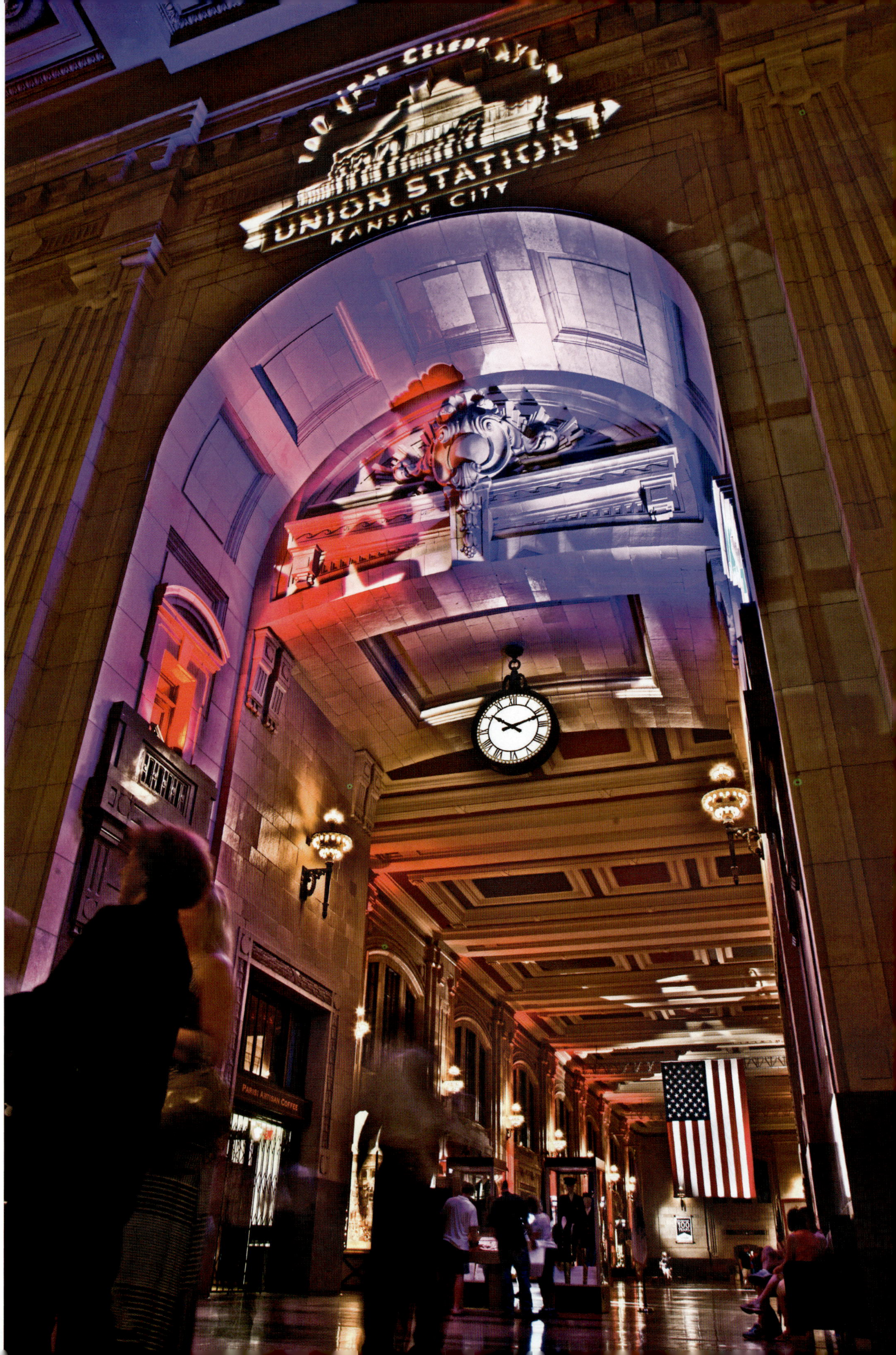
UNION STATION
KANSAS CITY

115

Memorial Day, Far Left – *Colored gels created a patriotic display for Memorial Day 2014.*

Star Plotting, Left & Below – *The curved ceiling that partially surrounds the Grand Stairs on the Theatre Level was once an open planetarium. A local astronomy group plotted constellations onto overhead transparency material as the stars and planets would have appeared the night of the station's opening in 1914. Those points were transferred to the ceiling material by a Capital Electric technician; tiny holes of varying diameters were drilled at the points so that light would shine through, simulating the heavens. The overall hue of the ceiling changed color as the day progressed, from early morning pinks and purples, to light blue at noon, and finally to a deep navy in the evening. Over the years since the restoration, the lighting has become non-functional. The ceiling was digitally retouched to show approximately how it once looked. Oddly, there was never an explanatory text block near the display to explain to the visitor what it was, so few people outside the original staff looked up or even knew.*

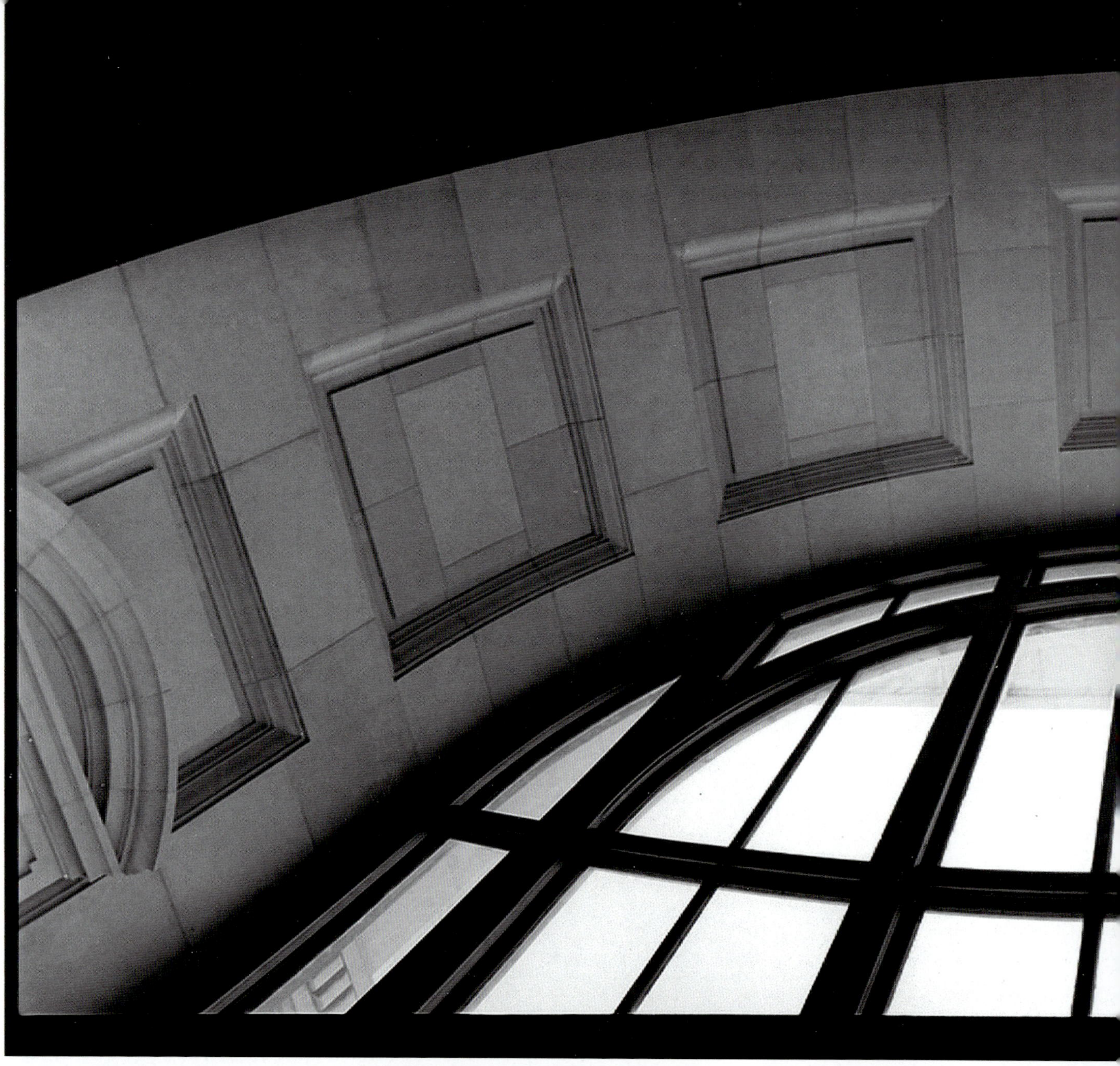

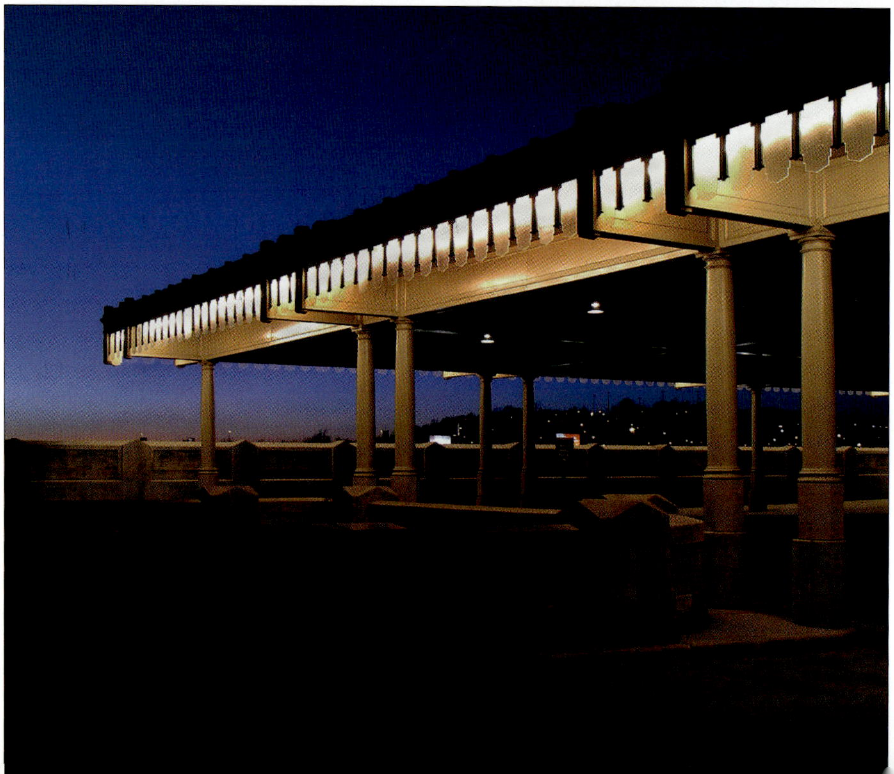

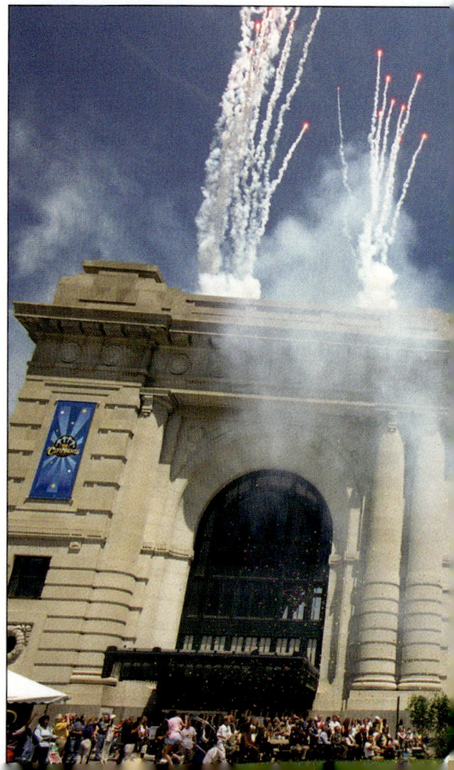

On The Road - *The Union Pacific #844 steam locomotive from the 1940s, shown on pages 100/101, pulled a long line of UP Armour Yellow passenger cars, including this classic, beautifully restored end car, as the train departed Union Station May 31, 2011. In a nod to yesteryear, the conductor waved farewell to Kansas City.*